The Channel Islands
Occupation and Liberation
1940 - 1945

The Channel Islands
Occupation and Liberation
1940 - 1945

Asa Briggs

B T Batsford Ltd • London
Published in association with the Imperial War Museum

ISBN 0 7134 7822 5

A CIP record for this book is available from the British Library

First published in Great Britain in 1995 by
B.T. Batsford Ltd
4 Fitzhardinge Street
London W1H 0AH

Printed in Great Britain
by Butler and Tanner, Frome, Somerset

At his ease: a German corporal
outside Headquarters

Contents

Maps

The geography of the Channel Islands in relation to England and France

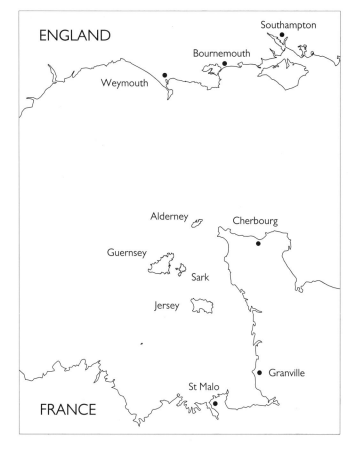

ENGLAND

Southampton
Bournemouth
Weymouth

Alderney
Cherbourg
Guernsey
Sark
Jersey
Granville
St Malo

FRANCE

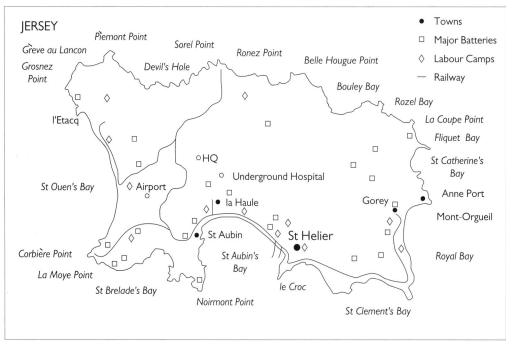

JERSEY

- Towns
- Major Batteries
- Labour Camps
- Railway

Piemont Point
Grève au Lancon
Sorel Point
Ronez Point
Grosnez Point
Devil's Hole
Belle Hougue Point
Bouley Bay
Rozel Bay
l'Etacq
La Coupe Point
Fliquet Bay
HQ
St Catherine's Bay
Underground Hospital
St Ouen's Bay
Airport
la Haule
Gorey
Anne Port
Mont-Orgueil
Corbière Point
St Aubin
St Helier
La Moye Point
St Aubin's Bay
Royal Bay
St Brelade's Bay
le Croc
Noirmont Point
St Clement's Bay

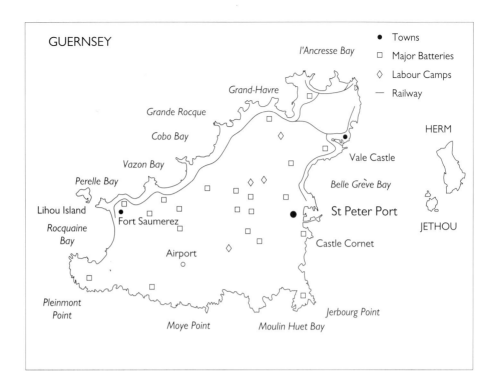

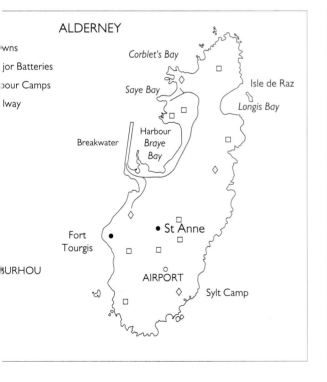

Foreword

The Channel Islands were the only British Isles to be occupied by the Germans during the Second World War which was fought on a global scale. This book tells the story fifty years later. Its first appearance coincided with the opening of a major special exhibition in the Imperial War Museum to mark the anniversary, a joint project with the Governments of Jersey and Guernsey, where parallel exhibitions were also being staged. It has been written, however, with a longer life in mind. In addition to recording what happened in the Islands it stimulates thoughts about what would have happened in the bigger island of Britain had the Germans invaded. It also inspires more profound thoughts about conflict and reconciliation.

On 30 June 1940, a Sunday, a German pilot, Hauptmann Liebe-Pieteritz, landed on Guernsey, establishing that it was undefended, and that evening Junkers transport planes carried in a *Luftwaffe* platoon. The island was occupied without resistance, although few people living there knew of it until they read their newspapers next morning. On 1 July 1940 Jersey was taken over after another German pilot had dropped surrender ultimatums telling citizens to hang out white flags. Operation *Grüne Pfeile*, 'Green Arrow', had been accomplished.

The news was announced to the British people in a brief statement issued by the Ministry of Information, which appeared in *The Times* on 2 July. Berlin radio had announced it earlier, and the BBC had broadcast a warning message from the Postmaster-General, at 7.20 pm on 1 July 1940, tucked away among what were called 'national and regional announcements', that 'all communication with the Channel Islands has been temporarily suspended, there was no reference to the occupation in the 9 pm news bulletin, high spot of the day, which was followed by a talk by R.H.S. Crossman on 'The Nazi Way'.

The Berlin radio message was more dramatic, and in characteristic Nazi

The Postmaster General announces that all ▓▓▓▓▓

communication with the Channel Islands has been temporarily

suspended. Telephone calls and telegrams cannot be accepted,

and letters and parcels for the islands should not be posted

pending a further announcement.

The first swastika over Jersey's Town Hall

The first Union Jacks - before liberation

way followed the lines of other victory messages broadcast during the *Blitzkrieg* weeks after the successful invasion of Holland, Belgium and France ended the 'phoney war'. Paris had fallen on 14 June, and the French government had capitulated eight days later. Cherbourg was in German hands. The 1 July broadcast stated triumphantly that 'on June 30 the British island of Guernsey was captured in a daring *coup de main* of the *Luftwaffe*. In an air fight a German reconnaissance plane shot down two Bristol Blenheim bombers. On July 1 the island of Jersey was occupied by surprise in the same manner.' This news was followed by battle music, including the song, '*Wir fahren gegen England*'. It seemed that England would be next.

Almost five years later, on the afternoon of 8 May 1945, Winston Churchill, who had become prime minister on 10 May 1940, announced to the world that 'our dear Channel Islands will be freed today', and Union Jacks were flown again - with German permission. The following day, 9 May 1945, after a formal German unconditional surrender at 7.14 am precisely, a British advance party on H.M.S. *Bulldog* landed at St Peter Port in Guernsey, and later in the day a pinnace swept into St Helier in Jersey carrying two naval officers and four seamen. That afternoon, British expeditionary forces landed from HMS *Campion* and HMS *Cosby* both in Guernsey and Jersey, with accompanying fly-pasts of RAF Mosquitoes and Mustangs. On 10 May the Union Jack was formally hoisted in the Royal

Baron von Aufsess, the chroni-
cler who dreamt of peace

Square in St. Helier and the national anthem was sung. The main
Operation *Nestegg* force sailed from Plymouth on 11 May.

Surrounding these bare facts concerning the beginning and ending of
five years of subjection of British people on British soil there are thousands
of stories. One of them (by Frank Stroobant) is called, as all the stories
might have been, *One Man's War*. It took him out into Germany itself. 'We
seem to have lived half a lifetime in the last fortnight', one letter writer in
Guernsey, Dorothy Higgs, explained near the beginning on 2 July 1940.
At the end when Frank Falla returned to Guernsey from a German prison
camp on 27 July 1945 (his crime had been to listen to BBC news bulletins)
he 'fought to keep back the tears and control the lump' in his throat as he
'leaned over the side [of SS *Hantonia*] to soak in the beauty that was my

Commemoration: the fiftieth
anniversary of deportation

island home'.

Different storytellers have presented stories which more than one of
them have called 'fantastic'. Yet some stories were down-to-earth, for
many Channel Islanders kept diaries at the time, and Leslie Sinel of the
Jersey Evening Post prepared an invaluable day-by-day chronicle, leaving out
'the fantastic rumours which were continually in circulation in a rumour-
infested island'. Many of the diaries kept by Channel Islanders – and some
of them were abandoned half way through – have not been published: all
of them reveal through detail, often colourful, sometimes grim, how private and public lives intersected. One of the last books to appear in English
was the translation of the German diary of a German civil administrator,
Platzkommandant Baron von Aufsess. It covers the last phases of the occupation from a German angle. From the British angle there was only one
dominant theme, however it was expressed – liberation.

There was, of course, a prelude and an epilogue to all the wartime stories, the prelude misty and confused, the epilogue, still incomplete, but
revealing in itself. The prelude is well covered in the official history of the
occupation of the Islands, written by Charles Cruickshank, who was
selected by the then Director of the Imperial War Museum as its author.
Published in 1975, the history describes, but does not excuse, the early
confusion in the weeks preceding the Germans' arrival. The epilogue,
which Falla begins to chronicle in his book, *The Silent War* (1967), can
best be traced subsequently in the pages of the *Channel Islands Occupation
Review*.

As the events of the war have receded, the individual stories – and the
general story – have been reflected upon in retrospect, and a new genera-
tion has emerged for whom what happened is not experience but history.
Meanwhile, new evidence has been uncovered. The *Review* has drawn on
German as well as British evidence, written, oral and visual, and it has
applied proper critical standards in reviewing every new book on the

occupation that has appeared inside or outside the Channel Islands. Most of these books are listed on pages 91 to 93. The Society has also examined and restored fortifications, the subject of much detailed study, documentary and archaeological. Until the 1970s these were thought of as scars. Now they have become tourist attractions. The aim of the Society throughout has been 'actively to promote reconciliation and understanding between former enemies', an aim which large numbers of other Channel Islanders have come to share. To mark the fiftieth anniversary of the deportation of 2,400 non-native Channel Islanders to internment camps in Germany beginning on 15 September 1942 a commemorative service was held in 1992 at 2.30 pm, the very time that the deportation order had appeared in the *Jersey Evening Post*. It took place in the yard behind the

'They are putting up barbed wire everywhere.' Through barbed wire: the land. For the sea, see page 8.

Tourism Office in St. Helier. The lesson was read by a clergyman who had himself been deported at the age of three. Among those present was the Burgermeister of Wurzach, where some of the deportees had been held in the *Schloss*. 'Any former deportee who returned to Bad Wurzach today', he said, 'is always certain of a warm welcome.'

My own brief account of the occupation years, which takes account of changes in attitudes in the Channel Islands and in Britain since 1945, is no

Sounds of music: a German band plays in Alderney. 'It is amazing to see how rapt the German soldier is over Beethoven.'

Other sounds of music: a British band plays in Guernsey

substitute for the existing literature, a literature in layers. Nor, indeed, given its short length, can it be an adequate summary of it. It does not deal in detail with recently released official papers. Instead it seeks to put the experience of the occupation into historical perspective. The words 'experience' and 'perspective' do not always go easily together. They do, however, in this book which draws necessary contrasts between peaceful pre-war and post-war years and occupation years that broke many continuities. The history of the Channel Islanders is far longer than this century. It stretches back to prehistoric times, long before the Islands passed into the hands of the British Crown when William the Conqueror successfully invaded England in 1066.

The best way of relating experience to perspective for those not born in the Channel Islands is to visit them today and study on the spot what still remains: and Appendix 1 on page 89 give guidance on what to look for. Some of the surviving evidence speaks for itself: much of it requires explanation, and in Appendix 3 I have given the names of some of the people who through their explanations have helped me to understand. I am still learning. There is no substitute for talking to Channel Islanders who remember what happened, sometimes when they were very young. The barbed wire still guards the past. Many people for long wanted to forget. They object now to the 'hi-jacking' of their history by people who in seeking headlines succeed not so much in understanding as in simplifying and sensationalizing at the same time. Meanwhile, the music of wartime lingers: it echoes in many memoirs.

If one of the two necessary factors to consider in establishing perspective is history, the other is geography. Jersey and Guernsey are very different from each other both geographically and historically, and they remain deeply conscious of their differences. Jersey has an area of 45 square miles and Guernsey 24 square miles. There were about 50,000 people in Jersey in 1939 and about 40,000 in Guernsey. The constitutions of the Islands were as different as their sizes, but both were traditional in structure and flavour. Both islands had Lieutenant-Governors. Both had Bailiffs, appointed by the Crown, who were the links between the Lieutenant-Governors and the administrative departments: they chaired the Islands' ancient representative bodies, known as 'the States'. Most British people are unaware of these details. To the Germans the Islands in a graphic phrase were a 'constitutional nature reserve'.

To complete the picture, which would otherwise be incomplete, there are four main Channel Islands to consider, not two, Alderney, the Island nearest to England - and to France - and Sark, the smallest of the four. Each had its own highly distinctive war-time history. Alderney, twice as big in size (2,000 acres) as Sark, had a population of 1,500, Sark 600. The smaller islands, particularly Herm, Jethou and Lihou, cannot be left out of the picture either. The Germans examined them carefully when they arrived; British missions landed there. Administratively all these Islands were linked to the Bailiwick of Guernsey.

Alderney had been almost totally evacuated on 29 June 1940 before two German planes landed there on 2 July and cleared the runway. By contrast,

Feudal obedience: the Dame of
Sark

few inhabitants left Sark where a small German detachment arrived on 4
July, 'Personally', wrote Sybil Hathaway, *La Dame de Serk*, who had ruled
the Island in feudal fashion since 1926, 'I remain unless ordered to leave
and the Sarkese remain also'.

That was the beginning: what happened at the end was different also.
Alderney was officially liberated on 16 May, but those of its citizens who
returned later in the year found an island that was devastated and derelict.
The most British of the Islands had been the most German. When the
largest complement of returning Islanders, 115, got back on 15 December,
the Salvation Army Band played 'There's no place like home'.

Seven months earlier, on 10 May 1945 a German motor boat with three
British officers and twenty men had arrived in Sark, where they found
everything in good order; and when the senior British officer told Dame
Hathaway, who had hoisted the Union Jack two days earlier, that he could
not immediately spare any men, she herself agreed to watch over the 275
German troops who still remained there. 'As I have been left for nearly five
years', she told him, 'I can stand a few more days.' She remained in command of the German forces on Sark for six days, and all her orders were
obeyed: '*Zu befehl, gnädige Frau*'.

Full circle. A German jetty constructed in Alderney, to be
used for Hitler's invasion of
Britain, was demolished in 1979.
German prisoners–of–war
embarked for Britain here in
1945

SUMMER 1939 TIME TABLE

EFFECTIVE FROM 5TH MAY UNTIL 30TH SEPTEMBER

GUERNSEY AIRWAYS

GUERNSEY
FOR SUNSHINE

ONE The last summer

Travel by sea

Travel by air

The Channel Islands were islands of peace on 3 September 1939 when Britain declared war on Germany. Yet the Islanders were mentally, if not physically, prepared for war. 'At Last' was the headline in the *Jersey Evening Post* the following day. Two days before the declaration of war the Lieutenant-Governors of Jersey and Guernsey, without instructions from London, had ordered the call-up of all ranks in their armed militias, their traditional agencies of defence.

That was clear enough. There were signs of confusion, however, as well as of determination in September 1939; and these were more obvious in Whitehall than in St Helier or St Peter's Port. Home Office and War Office were not in close touch with each other, and the War Office, ultimately responsible for the defence of the Islands, found it necessary at this critical point, late in history, to ask questions concerning 'the machinery by which we communicate with the Lieutenant-Governors [both military men] in their capacity as General Officers Commanding'. 'Could one deal with them direct, or had all communications to go through the Home Office?'

Neither the War Office nor the Home Office - nor indeed the communications system - came out well in dealings which concerned the Channel Islands during the phoney war. Indeed, what happened during these months has been described by Cruickshank in carefully chosen words as 'a slow moving comedy of administrative errors'. Orders arrived late: sometimes they were contradictory.

Germany, too, despite the fact that it was a dictatorship, did not find it easy to deal with departmental rivalries and overlaps, and there were sharp differences of outlook and ambition between the Army, the Navy and the Airforce which were apparent even before the fate of the Channel Islands lay in their hands. There was ample evidence later of administrative incompetence also. Unworkable orders had more than once to be rescinded. Yet in June 1943 a German official was to indulge in self-praise and claim that since 1940 'the face of the Islands' had become 'more serious and more European', and that they would have 'their place and mission in the new Europe'.

During the phoney war the Channel Islands made a substantial financial contribution to the British war effort. Already in the summer of 1939 Guernsey had voted £180,000 towards the cost of the defence of the Island, doubling its income tax in order to do so, and in March 1940 Jersey raised a loan of £100,000 as a 'first instalment'. Lord Portsea, who was doughtily to defend the interests of the Channel Islands from London during the darkest years of the war, calculated in a letter to *The Times* that a proportionate amount from the United Kingdom would be £118 million.

The Complete Flight

After 3 September 1939 daily life had gone on much the same as before in the Channel Islands, and during the spring of 1940 tourists were still arriving by boat in Jersey, which in 1939 had a larger tourist industry than Guernsey, proud of its new airport opened that year. 'War time holidays' were on offer, and the Jersey Tourism Committee resolutely answered the question 'Is it right to take your holidays in war time?' with a statement that

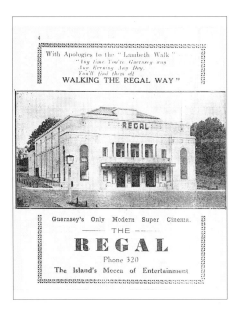

4

With Apologies to the " Lambeth Walk "
" Any time You're Guernsey way
Any Evening Any Day.
You'll find them all
WALKING THE REGAL WAY "

Guernsey's Only Modern Super Cinema.
THE
REGAL
Phone 320
The Island's Mecca of Entertainment

The Regal Way

it called 'the official view': '...money is well spent on annual holidays, since the individual returns to his work refreshed mentally and physically and ready to give of his best in the interests of the national war effort.' 'Why Jersey?' it went on. Because it offered 'an ideal solution. ...Situated as it is in the English Channel and sheltered by France' it was 'the ideal resort for wartime holidays. Happily our Island is far removed from the theatre of war. The bays with their eternal sands, sea and sunshine, together produce an atmosphere of peaceful tranquillity strangely different from the rest of the world.' As late as 22 June 1940 *The Times* quoted a tourist advertisement for a group of hotels recommended by Ashley Courtney. Another advertisement (complete with telephone number) recommended the St Brelade's Hotel as 'the safest place on earth'.

Closeness to France scarcely provided shelter, let alone safety, as German forces burst through western Europe in ideal holiday weather during the early summer of 1940. Nor did the word 'eternal' continue to have quite the same ring about it when every day brought news of new German triumphs. The atmosphere was uneasy and uncertain, and Leslie Sinel wrote in his chronicle of queues forming outside the railway booking offices and of English residents leaving in haste. There was also a run on the banks. In Guernsey a curfew was imposed on 3 June from 10 pm to 6 am for all inhabitants except those of British and French nationalities: significant numbers of foreign, including Irish, workers were living there.

In London two radically contrasting decisions were taken by the War Cabinet on the morning and afternoon of 12 June. In the morning the Cabinet, advised by the Chief of the Imperial General Staff, approved the sending of two battalions, one to Jersey, one to Guernsey. In the afternoon the same Cabinet, advised by the Secretary of State for War, proposed that in view of the fact that the Germans would soon reach the nearby French coast the battalions should not be sent.

What you could see on the screen

Demilitarization of the Islands was the inevitable consequence. The formal decision to take it on 19 June followed its implicit acceptance days before. At the very top Churchill did not like the reasoning behind the decision, but he could do nothing to prevent the decision being taken. Thereafter communications difficulties increased. Neither of the Lieutenant-Governors - and a new Lieutenant-Governor arrived in Guernsey as late as 4 June - was kept well-informed. They could communicate with Whitehall, but the officials at the other end of the telephone line were at best soothing, at worst misleading. Not surprisingly, on 19 June, the day when it was decided to begin evacuations, `wild rumours' were circulating.

Evacuation and the problems that it posed are dealt with in the next chapter. There could be no demilitarization, however, before the evacuation, and on 21 June after the evacuation had been carried out, the two Lieutenant-Governors left. The Chiefs of Staff now asked the Foreign Office to inform the German Government through diplomatic channels that demilitarization was complete. The Home Office accordingly prepared a statement, but the Foreign Office took no immediate action, and the statement was withheld. On 24 June the Bailiffs, who had taken over the powers of the Lieutenant-Governors, received an unsigned message from King George VI. It began with the words:

> For strategic reasons it has been found necessary to withdraw the armed forces from the Channel Islands. I deeply regret this necessity and I wish to assure my people that in taking this decision my Government has not been unmindful of their position. It is in their interest that this step should be taken in present circumstances.

For those with a knowledge of ancient history (and there were several such people in the Channel Islands) this message must have recalled, in tone and in content, a message sent centuries before by the Roman Emperor Honorius telling the British that Rome could no longer protect them and asking them to look after their own interests.

There was one big difference, however. King George's message ended with the more comfortable, if not entirely comforting, words that

> The link between us will remain unbroken and I know that my people in the Islands will look forward with the same confidence as I do to the day when the resolute fortitude with which we face our present difficulties will reap the reward of victory.

Again communications proved faulty. This unsigned royal message was never circulated. The Home Secretary had passed it on with the qualifying words that the message was 'for communication to the people in such manner as may seem to you advisable having regard to the interests of national security'.

In 1940, when Britain stood alone against the might of Germany, the claims of 'national security' obviously came first. But the claims were seldom thought through intelligently. Demilitarization was not announced to the enemy on the grounds that it would be inopportune to do so, indeed that it would be in German interests; and when a Member of Parliament put down a question on the subject at Westminster on 28 June he was asked to withdraw it. The Germans never learned officially, therefore, and on that same day, a week after the Lieutenant-Governors had left, there were German air raids on unprotected Guernsey and Jersey. It was not until the morning of 29 June that the Home Office released the news of the bombings and at the same time of the Islands' 'demilitarization'. It was too late.

The Attorney General of Guernsey, Ambrose (later Sir Ambrose) Sherwill, was on the telephone to the Home Office in London when the Guernsey raid took place on the harbour: 29 people were killed. There was a note of horror in the scene in St Peter Port, where the Germans mistook tomato lorries for ammunition convoys: blood mingled with tomato pulp at the quayside, and cattle, just brought in from Alderney, plunged loose. In the Jersey raid nine people were killed. The last official communication with London was a telegram to the Home Office.

Behind the scenes there was also German confusion during the last stages of the prelude. On 18 June the German Admiral in command in France, Karlgeorg Schuster, appropriately a future head of the German Naval History Branch, was discussing how best to capture the Islands, not knowing that decisions were being taken to demilitarize them; and after ordering reconnaissances, he continued to believe, even when confronted with photographic evidence, that German forces would meet stiff opposition. He envisaged a combined operation, therefore, *Grüne Pfeile*, which would involve naval assault troops, the *Wehrmacht* and the *Luftwaffe*. It was while in Paris on 30 June explaining the Navy's costly plan at a strategic conference that he learned that Hauptmann Liebe-Pieteritz had landed without opposition in Guernsey. The first triumph in what might have been a Channel Islands war was the victory of the *Luftwaffe* over the German Navy.

TWO Evacuation

In the hands of the police:
'somewhere in Glasgow'

Following the decision to demilitarize the Channel Islands one day after the German armies reached Cherbourg, civilian as well as military evacuations began; and no fewer than 22,656 citizens were taken away from the Islands in five days, about a fifth of the population of Jersey and about half the population of Guernsey. It was a deeply disturbing experience both for those who left in haste and for those who stayed behind. 'Everywhere' the evacuees were asking the same question, 'Where shall we go? And none could answer.' This was how one of the evacuated men from Guernsey recalled the evacuation two years later in the pages of the *Channel Islands Monthly Review*, published far away from home in industrial Stockport.

Britain was billeting 35,000 refugees from the European continent during the hot summer of 1940, when the Channel Islanders, about a third of the total population, arrived by boat in Weymouth. Evacuation of the Islands had been considered before the war, but no plans for it had ever been made. It was only on 16 June that they began to be taken seriously after the Home Office, the Department responsible, took it for granted that the Islands would be abandoned to their fate. C.G. Markbreiter, the civil servant in charge, gave the news to Jurat Dorey, who represented Jersey and Guernsey on an unhappy mission to London on 18 June.

The news of impending evacuation created consternation when it was taken back to the Islands by Dorey, and although it was announced in the local press on 19 June that ships would be provided to evacuate women and

The press announces
simultaneously evacuation and
demilitarization

children, men between 20 and 33 who wished to join the Forces, and, if possible, other men, the Lieutenant-Governor of Jersey reported by telephone to London on the following day that the piers were crowded with people and that there were signs of panic. The evacuation was not completed by the time that he and his opposite number, both military men, were themselves recalled to London, handing over control of the islands to the Bailiffs and the officers of the Crown.

The circumstances and procedures of evacuation varied in the different islands. So, too, did the atmosphere and the outcomes. In Jersey the Bailiff, A.M. (later Lord) Coutanche, gave a lead. Addressing a large crowd in the Royal Square, he advised most people to stay. 'I will never leave', he told them, 'and my wife will be by my side.' In Guernsey, the first announcement on 19 June that children of school age, younger children accompanied by their mothers, and 'all others' should register for evacuation that evening created immediate confusion, not made easier the following day when a local anti-evacuation campaign gained strength. The Bailiff was silent, and Sherwill, who was placed in authority, was no more certain about what to do than his fellow citizens. One of them, 64-year-old J.C. de Sauvary, who had not yet started to write a diary, changed his mind more than once about whether to leave the island or to stay. In the end, however, in his own words he 'did not have the choice, events happened too quickly'. When the evacuation of children began at 6 am on 20 June, embarking children got mixed up with disembarking troops, and it was 2.30 in the afternoon before the last of the children went on board.

What happened in Alderney was in sharp contrast with what happened both in Jersey and Guernsey. Brigadier F.G. French, Judge of Alderney, who had found it difficult to contact the Guernsey authorities, drafted hastily a handwritten notice on 22 June 1940 announcing that he had

Brigadier French's handwritten announcement of evacuation, Alderney

A first view of London

Where shall we go? Arriving at Weymouth

appealed directly to the Admiralty 'for a ship to evacuate us'. He also addressed a public meeting ending with the words 'Do we go or do we stay? Whatever we do, let's all do the same. Let's go together or stay together.' 'Let's go' was the general response. There was confusion in Alderney too, however, for it was not until 4.35 am on 23 June, an intim-

Prams arrive in Stockport

An old countryman discovers a
new land

idating time, that the church bells rang out warning the people to leave
their homes. It was noon before the last ship sailed.

In all three islands, particularly Alderney, animals, including pets, suffered terribly at the time of evacuation. In Jersey over five thousand cats
and dogs were killed in five days at the Animal Shelter. In Alderney cattle and pigs were left shut up and without food, and larger numbers of
cows were abandoned unmilked. When a rescue team arrived from
Guernsey on Tuesday 25 June they were appalled at what they found. In

A new nurse: Eastbrook Hall,
Bradford

Ballroom turned dormitory: 'somewhere in the North of England'

Taking exercise: nuns show evacuees a Lancashire park

the main street of St Anne's, the main island community, lay the body of a horse which had broken its neck trying to jump over a fence.

The evacuated men, women and children suffered too, although they often showed remarkable cheerfulness in the face of adversity. Some of them had hurried away in such haste that they left behind untidy houses and abandoned cars. After reaching Weymouth, the first port of entry, they dispersed by train, without much guidance, on tiring journeys to various parts of the country, north and south, men of military age to join the Forces, the rest to find employment. Children, separated from their parents, faced totally new experiences.

Conditions at the points of arrival varied, as did the warmth of the reception, but even where there was warmth there was an inevitable sense of shock. A refugee, who reached Bradford after a journey of more than

36 hours, felt that it was impossible 'to tell these kind folk that I thought I'd been dropped in the Black Hole of Calcutta'. Bradford was one of several reception posts in Lancashire, Cheshire and the West Riding to which many of the Islanders went.

Voluntary organization then and later was more sustaining than official action, but for many evacuees, more concerned about the plight of those they had left behind than about their own, religion was the main consolation: these were days of prayer. It was not until March 1941 that they

Telling a story to pass the time

Making their own story: 30 Guernseymen evacuate themselves in darkness in a motor launch and arrive in Dartmouth, July 1940

received Red Cross messages from their families at home.

Two letters which were posted in June 1940 by parents left behind in Jersey to their son and daughter-in-law in England never arrived: they were returned bearing the words NO POSTAL SERVICE scrawled on them and were found 34 years later. One of them, dated 27 June 1940, included the sentence,

> Most of the younger elements have left so that when, if ever, Jerry comes along he will find what is practically an Island of aged and cripples.

The second, dated 30 June, described the German air raid before the Germans arrived.

> The more we think about you [it went on], the more we are convinced that it was right for you to go. In fact, there are moments when doubt almost assails me that it would have been just as wise for us all to have crossed and then I think again that it was best for us to remain and stand firm and calm until the day comes when happier times will again smile upon us.

The same day the Germans arrived.

After two years of separation and exile, a very long time in the protracted history of the war, one of the people who had been evacuated in 1940 meditated on what had then happened. He had already acquired his own sense of perspective:

> The lapse of time permits a more detached view to be taken of the events of those memorable days. Helpless under the shadow of impending disaster, the responsibility of those in authority was undesirable. That mistakes were made is undeniable, no one is infallible. Probably more people could have left the islands with advantage to future food supplies and the public health.... Nevertheless, the facts are not known, and charity demands that we think with tolerance of those tragic occurrences and fateful decisions; that we suspend judgement for the time being at any rate - if not indefinitely.

The spirit of this writer was unbroken; and by the time that he wrote the collective spirit of the evacuees had been demonstrated in many different ways and in many different places, including towns and cities in Scotland. Fifty years later - and in far longer perspective - the *Guernsey Evening Press* was to run a series of articles based on reminiscences of the schoolchildren who had been evacuated in 1940, and not far from Stockport the town of Oldham was to hold a jubilee exhibition, 'We'll Meet Again'.

Whenever evacuees settled in a provincial town or city they set up a committee which organized a programme of social events, including lectures and lantern shows; and a reunion was held once a year. There were also large committees in Bath, Bristol, Exeter and Leicester. The activities of the different groups were recorded, often movingly, in the *Channel Islands Monthly Review*, which described itself as 'a Journal of Channel Island

Refugees'. Whatever news could be gleaned of what was happening in the Channel Islands was put into print, while information about Channel Islanders in exile, including those who had escaped, was supplied largely by the readers themselves, who were also granted their own platform.

The first volume of the *Review* covered the months from May to October 1941. It engaged in a continuing effort both to provide information and to keep morale high. The 'thought for the month' in August 1942 was the Biblical text, 'Wait on the Lord; be of good courage, and he shall … renew thy strength.'

National organization was provided through the Channel Islands Refugee Committee, staffed by volunteers and chaired by Lord Justice du Parcq, a Jerseyman. The Committee raised funds to relieve distress, and helped the first evacuees to find jobs and to deal with their personal problems. It also set up a Legal Advice Bureau. The last wartime address of the Committee in London – and of a separate Alderney Committee – was as fashionable as it could have been – 20 Upper Grosvenor Street. Yet the addresses of most of the scattered Channel Islanders – and 30,000 of them were said to have passed through the Committee's hands – were far from fashionable. There were many, too, who were serving in the Forces, and a register of them was carefully kept. There was a room in Grosvenor Street, called 'Le Coin' (the corner) for Channel Islanders passing through London. It was a home from home.

Who can resist ice cream?

THREE Occupation

On 20 June 1940 German Navy Group West had received the order, 'Occupation of the British Channel Islands...is urgent and important. Carry out local reconnaissance and execution thereof.' It was not until 30 June, however, that occupation began. On the same Sunday, far away in the east of Europe, where Germany and Russia were not yet locked in war with each other, Soviet airborne forces landed behind the Romanian frontier in Bessarabia. They too were unopposed.

East and West can never be separated from each other in dealing with the wartime story of the Channel Islands, particularly after the Germans invaded the Soviet Union in June 1941. The first German troops to land in Jersey and Guernsey, Infantry Division 216 – and they were not handpicked for the task – were to be switched to the eastern front, and many of them were to be killed there, among them Major Albrecht Lanz, first Military Commandant. Some German soldiers, injured on the Eastern Front, were to be sent to the Channel Islands rather than discharged.

The German ultimatum to the Channel Islands on 1 July 1940 included the words, 'In case of peaceful surrender the lives, property and liberty of peaceful inhabitants are solemnly guaranteed.' Like all Hitler's solemn guarantees, this was to be broken. Yet after the air raids the occupation began peacefully enough.

Soon after the second *Luftwaffe* landing on Guernsey at 7.30 pm on 30 June Inspector Sculpher of the Guernsey Police handed over to the senior

Enter the Luftwaffe

Translation of a Communication addressed to the
Governor of the Isle of Jersey.

1st July, 1940.

**To the Chief of the Military and Civil
Authorities**

Jersey (St. Helier).

1. I intend to neutralize military establishments in Jersey by occupation.

2. As evidence that the Island will surrender the military and other establishments without resistance and without destroying them, a large White Cross is to be shown as follows, from 7 a.m. July 2nd, 1940.

   a. In the centre of the Airport in the East of the Island.
   b. On the highest point of the fortifications of the port.
   c. On the square to the North of the Inner Basin of the Harbour.

   Moreover all fortifications, buildings, establishments and houses are to show the White Flag.

3. If these signs of peaceful surrender are not observed by 7 a.m. July 2nd, heavy bombardment will take place.

   a. Against all military objects.
   b. Against all establishments and objects useful for defence.

4. The signs of surrender must remain up to the time of the occupation of the Island by German troops.

5. Representatives of the Authorities must stay at the Airport until the occupation.

6. All Radio traffic and other communications with Authorities outside the Island will be considered hostile actions and will be followed by bombardment.

7. Every hostile action against my representatives will be followed by bombardment.

8. In case of peaceful surrender, the lives, property, and liberty of peaceful inhabitants are solemnly guaranteed.

    The Commander of the German Air Forces in Normandie,

                          General

The States have ordered this Communication to be printed and posted forthwith, and charge the inhabitants to keep calm, to comply with the requirements of the Communication and to offer no resistance whatsoever to the occupation of the Island.

All surrender!

Top right. Formality: the first official meeting in Guernsey (Ambrose Sherwill greets Maas and Lanz)

In control: Major Lanz (centre), first German Commandant

More formality: the first official meeting in Jersey (Bailiff Coutanche, second from left)

The Dame of Sark receives her German guests

They sign her visitors' book

On the march: into St Helier

On parade: Guernsey,
October 1940

Luftwaffe officer a letter signed by the Bailiff, Victor Carey, and addressed to the Officer commanding the German troops: Guernsey, he explained, was an 'open island'; no forces of any kind were stationed there. The following day, Lanz met the Bailiff and a newly made swastika flag, commissioned from a local dealer the previous day, was hoisted over the signal mast of the terminal. It was Jersey's turn next. After a reconnaissance, Lanz flew on to St Helier carrying the flag with him, and there too the bailiff surrendered officially. The swastika flag now flew over Jersey also.

Verboten: no photographs
here!

Islanders were required to
identify themselves

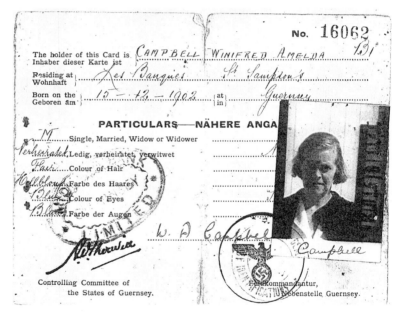

The Naval Assault Group, which had moved in after the *Luftwaffe*,
quickly returned to Paris, and Infantry Division 216 arrived in the Islands.
Looking at distant Alderney from France before the Division arrived, Lanz
thought that it 'would be a great idea for us to land over there'; and one
of his fellow officers, fully agreeing with him, added that he had already
asked 'why should we not cross over and occupy these beautiful Channel
Islands - even those lying south of Alderney, Guernsey and Jersey.' After
the landings Lanz, who held the degree of Doctor of Law and Philosophy,
went on to write a report which not only set out facts but registered feelings. Describing his first meeting with the Bailiff of Guernsey, he remarked
that when with his arms folded 'the old gentleman bowed deeply before
the representatives of the German Army' this was 'the first time in the his-

The new command and the old

tory of England that...the direct representative of his Britannic Majesty has ever bowed to the German Army'.

Lanz observed that the Islanders as a whole were surprised that the German troops were behaving correctly: they had been taken in by British propaganda. But they also behaved correctly too, he thought. This was an unprecedented situation, but neither the Islanders nor the Germans expected that the Occupation would last long. It was to last, of course, for nearly five years and to go through many phases. Yet much was to continue to remain in place throughout the war even after the Islands had become a fortress and were under siege. The autonomous States of Jersey and Guernsey continued to meet, although both had delegated their powers to smaller executive bodies before the Germans arrived. German officials were present at all States meetings. The royal coat of arms and the portrait of the King remained on the wall. Edicts were issued with the German Commandant taking over the role of the King in Council, and they were published, as before the war, in the official *Gazettes*. Prayers continued to be said for the royal family and the British Empire. The police continued to function. So too did medical and other essential services. Supplies were brought in from France. Nonetheless, it was Hitler's

Illicit wireless sets included home-made crystal sets and tuning units in disguise

portrait that hung in the Commandant's office, and all the actions of the States were subject in varying degrees to German dictates.

On 1 August 1940 Sherwill, as head of Guernsey's Controlling Committee, recorded a broadcast for German radio which the Germans used for propaganda purposes. He was not speaking, he said, with a revolver pointed at his head. The German authorities had treated the Bailiff with courtesy, the conduct of the troops had been 'exemplary', the Island government was operating. 'Banks, shops and places of entertainment were open as usual.' So also were churches and chapels. Unemployment was low. This would-be reassuring message to Channel Islanders who had left their families behind did not appeal to all of them at a time when Britain itself was expecting invasion and the Battle of Britain was about to begin. And no such broadcast was made again.

Sherwill did not refer to what had happened and was happening in Alderney and Sark. The former was devastated - only fifteen people had remained; the latter had been occupied by only eleven soldiers. In April 1941, when a German marine artillery unit was brought into Alderney, they found what one German called a picture of wanton destruction. In the same year, however, crops began to be grown for the first time since evacuation.

In Jersey and Guernsey life was less horrifying than it was in Alderney and in several other countries under German occupation. Games were played, concerts were presented, services were held. Yet Sherwill's use of the words 'as usual' was an exaggeration even at the beginning. Transport was the first item to be affected. Bicycles - and horses - replaced cars and buses. Driving on the right became compulsory. Road signs appeared in German, and first voluntary and then compulsory German lessons were introduced to unwilling pupils in schools. The press was censored from the start, and after British reconnaissance raids in July 1940 on Guernsey, Operations *Anger* and *Ambassador*, radios were confiscated (to be restored again in time for Christmas).

Off duty: Sonderführer Herzog with dog and shrimping net (Alderney Harbour)

A German Christmas in Guernsey

Hitler's birthday 1942 (St
Peter Port)

The latest cinema attraction:
'Victory in the West'

NOTICE

FOR German films with
English sub-titles
the left-hand section of
the stalls are reserved
for Civilians only; the
right-hand section and
the Balcony for German
troops only.

Separation at the cinema
(sport was separated too)

Other big changes included the introduction of the Reichsmark and
of German time. Hotels now housed German soldiers and administra-
tors. There were far more rules and regulations, ensuring that much that
had been 'normal' now became illegal. The system lacked moral support.
Radios were kept illegally, for example, in the consoles of cinema organs
in both Jersey and Guernsey. The Guernsey radio was not discovered; the
Jersey organist's was, and he was deported.

The Islanders then and later always faced threats not only of individual punishment but of collective reprisal. No revolvers might be pointed
at the Bailiffs' heads, but as Jurat Leale (later Sir John Leale) pointed out
in an impressive and wide-ranging speech delivered to the States of
Guernsey after the war was over, 'if the velvet glove never entirely dis-

In the bookshop: Buston's
Corner. Books include *Famine
in England* and *The Decline and
Fall of the British Empire*

Two ways of moving around

appeared the iron glove beneath it was more prominent'. Leale, a
Methodist minister, took Sherwill's place on 30 December 1940 when the
latter was suspended by the Germans. He emphasized properly, after the
Islands had been liberated, that it would have been wrong to assume that
'if only one was firm enough the Germans would give way', making the
further point that 'we were not at liberty to explain many of our actions'.
The Islands had been isolated, but the Islanders and the Germans could
not be isolated from each other. They had to live side by side. Some of
the Germans made the very best of it. They enjoyed the landscape, the
seascape – and their leisure.

   Informers were the worst enemies of the Islanders, the enemy in their
own midst: and when N.V.L. Rybot prepared an occupation alphabet in

A third way: a bus converted
to run on charcoal

Requisitioning transport

STATES OFFICE,
SAUMAREZ PARK,
GUERNSEY

15 Oct 1940

Dear Sir/Madam,

      In conformity with the Order of the German
Authorities in relation to the requisition of Motor Vehicles
in this Island, you are hereby required to produce your
motor vehicle, Registered No. 106 at St Peter Port
Garage Rue du Pré
on Thursday, the 17 Oct at 9 am
complete with the documentary evidence required by the
Order.

      On the acquisition of the vehicle by the
German Authorities, they will hand to the owner or his
representative, a receipt stating the purchase price.

      This receipt must be transmitted to me at the
States Office, Saumarez Park, for subsequent settlement.

      Attached is a form of declaration which you
are required to complete and sign, and produce to the German
Authority when the vehicle is presented. This declaration
must be forwarded to me, with the receipt referred to in the
foregoing paragraph. The Registration Book relating to the
vehicle must, at the same time, be transmitted to me.

      Also enclosed is a Coupon to enable you to
obtain the quantity of petrol specified in the Order, for
the purpose of delivering the vehicle. This will be
delivered to you by Messrs. Leale Ltd. and the coupon must
be handed to Messrs. Leale's carman in exchange for the
petrol delivered.

      This letter constitutes an authority for the
vehicle to be on the roads for the purpose of delivery,
whether licensed or not.

Yours faithfully,

School

States Supervisor.

The fate of the ambulance

July 1944 he described informers quite accurately and (by then the war had turned) forecast their fate. 'I', he stated, for example,

> Is for Informers, a pestilent brood
> Their doom is impending, though hanging's too good.

It was an informer who betrayed the five men who ran GUNS, the Guernsey Underground News Service which provided transcripts of BBC news. They were imprisoned and two of them died. Yet none of the wartime informers was to be hanged. (In Sark the German Commandant had ignored a notice pinned to a tree listing the names of people who had not handed in their radios, declaring it to be the work of a 'traitor'. That was German 'honour'.) In dealing with informers steadfastness and imagination were necessary as well as bravery. Reg Blanchford operated the St John's Ambulance Brigade in Guernsey in what Carel Toms called 'a war of wits against the occupiers': Post Office sorters steamed open informers' letters.Under A in the alphabet another prevalent war-time sin was identified:

> A is for Avarice, one of our vices,
> We corner the goods and put up the prices.

During the war the black market thrived in all countries, occupied or unoccupied; and in the Channel Islands it was a main source of profit as prices soared. The price of black market meat, for example, rose from 11s a pound to 15s a pound between July 1942 and 1943 and that of sugar from 12s 6d to 16s. Food became scarcer and scarcer, and substitutes became necessities - acorn coffee, bramble leaf tea, potato flour. It was in the interest both of the German and the Island authorities to check the black market: it was a source of profit for Germans and Islanders alike.

A third target of the alphabet maker was not unique to the Channel Islands - sex with the occupying forces. German soldiers were not allowed to marry Channel Island girls. Those girls who slept with them were known as 'Jerry bags'. Guernsey, which had a high illegitimacy rate before

A B C D E F G H I J K L M N O P Q R S T U V W X Y Z

A, is for Avarice, one of our vices.
We corner the goods and put up the prices.

B, is the Bungler who fancied it funny
To feed us on olives, dried carrots and tunny.

C, is for Conchies, contemptible wights
Who prefer to make hay while the other man fights.

D, 's the Deported. Their terrible fate
Has fostered our fury and hardened out hate.

E, is for Eatables—things nice to eat,
Like the cabbage, the turnip, the spud and the beet.

F, stands for Feathers which, mingled with tar,
Will decorate Jerrybags after the war.

G, are the Gossips. Avoid them with care !
They repeat and exaggerate all that they hear.

H, is for Hunger which makes you feel faint.
Some farmers know nought of this common complaint.

I, 's for Informers, a pestilent brood.
Their doom is impending, though hanging 's too good.

J, is for Jersey, enchained by the foe,
And abandoned by Britain in nineteen four o.

K, is the Knockout. The prophets are sure
It will come with a crash in the year forty-four.

L, are those Letters, from which you can tell
That year before last all the senders were well.

M, are the Markets, wherein you may spy
The price-lists of things you're unable to buy.

N, are the Nastics, incredible devils,
But were they such poops as our Ramsays and Nevilles ?

O, is my Overdraft. Sad to disclose,
The blacker the market, the greater it grows.

P, 's Profiteers. Though the Cops know them all,
They leave them at large as the Prison 's too small.

Q, are the Queues. Some are endless, I fear.
If you queue for a fish you will queue for a year.

R, is the Reichsmark all crumpled and creased,
I have heard it described as the Mark of the Beast.

S, are the Stalwarts. Refusing to mope,
They hold to the adage " While life lasts, there 's hope."

T, is for Tummies,—no longer in vogue,
You may bet, if you see one, the owner 's a rogue.

U, 's Uniforms. How we long for the day
When Khaki replaces the filthy Field Grey.

V, stands for Vitamins, medicos' pets.
They abound in commodities nobody gets.

W, 's We. We're a nation of barmies
Who owned half the world but would not keep armies.

X, are Xchanges oft offered for " What."
A candle, a pram, and a shirt or a yacht.

Y, is our Yearning for bacon and ham,
Tea, sausages, soap, fish, sugar and jam.

Z, is for Zero. Soon, over the Mike
We'll be told that is all that is left of the Rike.

N. V. L. RYBOT,
July, 1944.

A German alphabet

Growing tobacco in Jersey: permits were required, and glasshouses were prohibited

the war (5.4 per cent), reached a peak of 21.8 per cent in 1944. Here too the alphabet maker had a warning to deliver:

> F stands for Feathers which mingled with tar
> Will decorate Jerrybags after the war.

In this instance also post-war punishments were unofficial and proved far less drastic than those carried out in liberated France. Jews did not figure in the alphabet: their fate was sealed in Berlin.

For one historian of the war, summing up, 'there were those who escaped, those who resisted, and those who collaborated, and one guesses that the population of Great Britain itself would have divided in much the same proportions after invasion.' In fact, there were few signs of ide-

Digging peat in Guersey

Friendly waters

ological collaboration with the Nazis. V-signs appeared in the early summer of 1941, and those Channel Islanders found scrawling them were
punished until the Germans found it more convenient to use V-signs
themselves. Nor were V-signs the only protest. One Guernsey woman,
Mrs Winifred Green, was sent to prison in Caen for four months for
uttering the words 'Heil Churchill' when she was working as a waitress
at the Royal Hotel.

Charges brought against recalcitrant Channel Islanders at the time
included insults (one man threw dung over a German officer), spreading
British propaganda, sheltering foreign workers, and sabotage. A charge

Friendly people

Making the most of
occupation

brought against the authorities long after the end of the war was that they
aided the Nazis in 'hunting down Jews'. In fact, they could not prevent
Jews from being identified. Refusal to obey German orders always carried
with it a degree of threat, and deportation not only of Jews but of non-
Channel Islanders by birth, which is described in the next chapter, shows
what could happen – and how. Some Channel Islanders dared to escape.

It was after the deportations that on two remarkable formal occasions
the people of both of the biggest Channel Islands demonstrated their own
depths of feeling. In June 1943 a military funeral for two RAF non-com-
missioned officers whose bodies had been washed ashore in Jersey was an

occasion when everyone came together. Crowds gathered along the routes to the cemetery. The coffins bore Union Jacks and wreaths presented both by the States and by the *Luftwaffe*: there were two lorry-loads of them. The *Luftwaffe* provided bearers and a firing party. In November 1943 it was the Navy's turn. After an unsuccessful operation, one of several, the bodies of eighteen crew members of the destroyed cruiser HMS *Charybdis* and of the destroyer HMS *Limbourn* were washed up on the shore of Guernsey, twenty-nine in Jersey and one in Sark. Mass funerals were held, and the German Commandant delivered an oration at the graveside. 'We honour them as soldiers. They did their duty for their country.' In Britain the *Daily Mail* was able to reproduce a picture of this funeral on 27 January 1944.

By then the Occupation was drawing to its close after the Islands had

Staying out

Resisting: Winifred Green, who shouted 'Heil Churchill' and was clapped into jail for six months, and her husband.

Jews were identified - and
deported, some to meet
death.

Honour could be observed:
the funeral of two RAF men in
Jersey

gone through phases of fortification and siege; and it was while fortification was still proceeding, that deportation in a series of grim episodes
brought new breaks and new sufferings.

News from England

No. 1   SEPTEMBER 1940   DISTRIBUTED BY THE R.A.F.

To The Channel-Islanders

All of you, His Majesty's loyal subjects on the Channel Islands, must keep asking yourselves two great questions :—" How long must we put up with the German occupation ? " and " How are our friends on the mainland ? "

This news-sheet brings you the heartening answers. We on the mainland are in good heart. By subjecting our women and children to the wickedest form of warfare known to history, Hitler has only stiffened our backs. And the events of the last three weeks have only served to confirm Mr. Churchill's words of August 21st, that " the road to victory may not be so long as we expect." Nor may the day be so distant when we shall come to your relief. All our rapidly and enormously increasing strength is directed towards that day when the shadow of the bully will be lifted from you and from the whole of Europe. We shall continue to bring you the news from England as often and as regularly as we can.

A MESSAGE FROM HIS MAJESTY THE KING

The Queen and I desire to convey to you our heartfelt sympathy in the trials which you are now enduring. We earnestly pray for your speedy liberation, knowing that it will surely come.

GEORGE R. I.

Bombs over Germany

Hitler has suffered his first major defeat. While the mass raids on Britain have been broken up at a devastating cost to the Luftwaffe, the Royal Air Force carries out nightly raids on Germany and the Occupied Territories with such precision and intensity that the Hitler war machine has been visibly weakened.

The attacks on Germany have now lasted three months. From the North Sea to the borders of Czechoslovakia, from the Baltic to the Swiss Frontier, there is no military objective which is safe from them. Across the Alps, too, heavy blows have been struck at such targets in Milan, Turin, Genoa and other industrial centres.

Only military targets are attacked, but the effect has been that much the more serious. It contrasts strikingly with the indiscriminate terror bombing over England carried out by pilots who lack the training for more damaging tactics.

In Berlin itself gasworks, power stations, armament factories and railway stations have been repeatedly and systematically bombed. Hamm, key terminus for Ruhr rail traffic, has been bombed over sixty times. The Dortmund-Ems Canal, another vital artery, has been pierced by the heaviest bombs and drained.

At Hamburg and Emden vast areas of the docks have been wiped out. Synthetic petrol installations at Stettin and Leuna, reservoirs at Kiel, power stations at Nuremberg and Munich have all felt the weight of the British fist.

The great German forests have been set on fire. In the Black Forest, the Harz and the forest of Thuringia outside Berlin, veils of flame have closed around hidden factories and munition stores until explosions broke out.

Besides these blows at the heart of Germany, the fortified ports in Norway, Holland, Belgium and France, where the Germans are concentrating for the suicidal attempt at invasion, have been repeatedly struck.

In Africa and Italian possessions in the Mediterranean a similar story has been written by the R.A.F. with the difference that the Italian anti-aircraft defences and fighting planes are weaker than the German.

UP AND UP

" Our production of aircraft already largely exceeds the enemy's." This important announcement was made by Mr. Winston Churchill on August 20th. " The American production is only just beginning to flow in," he added. " Our fighter and bomber strengths are now, after all this fighting, larger than they have ever been."

The Luftwaffe was then attempting to put our aircraft industry out of action. It was in vain. At the end of the month Lord Beaverbrook, Minister of Aircraft Production, was able to add his own statement to the Prime Minister's. He said :

" The men and women of the aircraft industry of Great Britain have provided for the R.A.F. in the last week more fighters and bombers than ever before in the history of aviation ".

A World against Germany

Large numbers of the new bombers shattering Germany and of the fighters defending our coasts will bear the names of cities thousands of miles away from Europe. Gifts have poured in from every continent.

A bomber and three fighters from British Guiana ; two Hurricanes from the Bahamas ; three hundred Spitfires from Ceylon ; fifty Spitfires from the Gold Coast ; seventy-five more from Hyderabad ; eighty more from East India ; twelve bombers from Malaya ; a bomber and two fighters from Mauritius ; two Spitfires from Mombasa ; £100,000 from New Zealand to be spent at Lord Beaverbrook's discretion ; ten Spitfires from Sarawak (and one from the Rajah) ; three bombers from Trinidad ; one Spitfire from St. Vincent and another from Granada in the Windward Isles ; four Spitfires from Zanzibar ; more fighters and bombers from Uganda ; more again from Rhodesia and a promise of regular monthly supplies ; more again still from Southern Rhodesia ; Spitfires yet again from the " Speed the Planes " fund in Natal ; large consignments of rupees from Madras.

All over the British Isles, meanwhile, individuals, groups of employees, towns and suburbs have presented Spitfires and Hurricanes to the nation. Every kind of group has subscribed, money has even come from people bearing the same christian name—the Harolds, the Georges, etc.

From everywhere come fighters and bombers, bombers and fighters, most of all Squadrons of Spitfires.

On the Rebound

By courtesy of 'The Star'

By courtesy of 'The Evening Standard'

IMPREGNABLE TARGET

Free France Rises Anew

Throughout the French Empire and in France itself there are signs that the spirit of France, which was temporarily numbed by the shock of defeat, is now re-awakening.

Immediately after the capitulation, General de Gaulle raised in England the banner of les Français libres. Then, on August 26th, all the French possessions in Central West Africa—the Chad, the French Cameroons, the French Congo and Oubangui-Chari—suddenly and with one accord rallied to the cause of Free France.

In those French possessions which are still under the domination of the Axis, there are signs of revolt. An unascertainable number of fighting planes from French Morocco have arrived at Gibraltar, piloted by French airmen who wish to fight with General de Gaulle. The French naval forces in the Mediterranean and at Djibuti are reported to be eagerly waiting for the moment when they can re-enter the war.

In France itself, where the Nazi boot presses most heavily, there are also signs of resurrection. The Vichy government has rejected the demand, presented by the Germans, for more than half the livestock in unoccupied France. The Germans, as they naturally tend to do, are over-reaching themselves in their greed and are provoking growing resistance. There is evidence of sabotage in the factories now working for Germany. The broadcasts of General de Gaulle are eagerly listened to, despite German threats of severe punishment. The time is not far off when in France, too, the revolt, which is still underground, will flame up into the open.

630

Where have all the flowers gone? High-ranking German officers inspect war graves.

THE BIRD-CAGE

MAC BRANDEL

ILAG VII
LAUFEN, OBERBAYERN-GERMANY
1944

FOUR Deportation

The Bird–Cage: the Laufen house journal

On 15 September 1942 a notice appeared in the Channel Islands press stating abruptly that:

> By order of Higher Authorities the following British subjects will be evacuated and transferred to Germany (a) Persons who have their permanent residence not on the Channel Islands, for instance, those who have been caught here by the outbreak of war (b) All those men not born on the Channel Islands and 16 to 70 years of age who belong to the English people, together with their families. Detailed instructions will be given by the Feldkommandantur 515.

1186 people were duly transported to Germany from Jersey alone, and there were further rounds of reprisal deportations in 1943. For the Nazis deportation was always part of a far bigger war-time picture. On 24 August 1942 the Germans began to deport Jews from unoccupied France with the support of the Vichy Government, and a trainload leaving Paris for concentration camps on 28 August included 150 children under the age of fifteen. By 5 September nearly ten thousand Jews had been rounded up.

The story of what happened in the Channel Islands had special features of its own, however, and deserves to be called 'fantastic'. In September 1941 nearly five hundred German civilians working in Iran had been arrested by the British authorities, and as a reprisal Hitler ordered that for every German held by the British ten residents of the Channel Islands who

Biberach: the Camp Orchestra

Tapestry made by Mrs D.O.
Aitkin while interned at
Biberach

had been born in the United Kingdom were to be deported. He asked also
for the names of any Iranians in the Islands: surprisingly, there was one.
The British who lived there, he raved, should be sent far away to the bleak
Pripet marshes in eastern Europe and their properties should be distributed among Channel Islanders of French descent.

Little happened for over a year: a further order was issued then to the
Bailiff of Jersey to arrange for 1200 British subjects to be deported; the
news came as a terrifying surprise to him and even to many Germans, who
called them 'evacuations'. The reason for the delay in implementing the
1941 order had been very similar to the reason for British slowness in
broaching earlier problems of evacuation in 1940 - departmental uncer-
tainty and interdepartmental confusion. The German Foreign Office was
involved as well as the *Wehrmacht*.

Coutanche protested strongly when he was ordered to name those who
were to go, and to instruct his Constables to serve them all with deportation notices. As a result, the Constables were not asked to carry out these
distasteful tasks. Yet the Germans did, many of them reluctantly. The first
batch of deported Britons left on 16 September, to be followed by a second batch on the 17th. On 21 September the States Council protested too,
pointing out that the order clashed with promises that the Germans
had made in 1940. Such protests were of no avail. To be British was
enough.

Five days later deportations from Guernsey started also, and no fewer
than 825 men, women and children left on the *Minotaur* on 26 and 27

Sketches of a room at
Biberach, by C. France

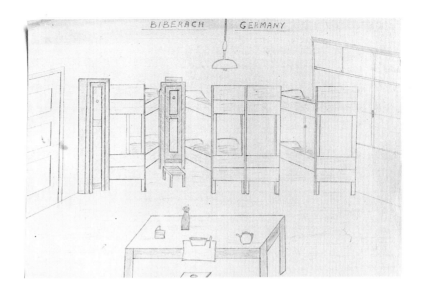

September. Nine people from Sark were deported with them. There
should have been eleven, but Major Shelton and his wife cut their wrists
to avoid being taken off: the Major died, his wife survived.

Letters telling those about to be deported from Guernsey what to do
said that they had to appear at the Gaumont Cinema, St Peter Port, at 3
pm on 26 September. They had to take with them 'warm clothes' (not
always easy), solid boots (far less easy), 'some provisions, meal-dishes,
drinking bowl and, if possible, a blanket'. 'Your luggage must not be heav-
ier than you can carry, and must bear a label with your full address.'

The people deported from the Channel Islands embarked on strange
journeys to unknown destinations. The first destination, although it was a
staging post, was Dorsten in the industrial Ruhr: it was located on a grim

GUERNSEY

Evening Press

Responsible Editor: J. S. IRISH.

No. 11,369   GUERNSEY, FRIDAY, OCTOBER 3, 1941   THREE-HALFPENCE

pital of Karelia
Finnish Troops

) Prisoners East of
iepr

German artillery fire, whilst another one was badly damaged.

Last night British bombers dropped a few high-explosive and incendiary bombs at random at several points in South-Western Germany. Only insignificant damage was caused.

During the successful battle against British supply shipping the German Navy and Air Force sank a total of 683,400 gross registered tons of enemy merchant shipping during the month of September. Of these 452,000 gross registered tons were destroyed by German submarines alone.

SPECIAL NEWSPAPERS FOR FOREIGN WORKERS IN GERMANY

The German Labour Front is planning to publish a special paper for Flemish workers in Germany. It is to be called "De Vlaamsche Post." At the same time a paper entitled "Van Honk" is to be published for the workers from the Netherlands. The Labour Front will then be publishing six papers for foreign workers in Germany. The first was the Italian paper "Il Camerata." "Le Pont," for French workers and Belgian Walloons, followed. The other foreign papers are for the Slovakian and the Danish workers in Germany. The papers appear once a week. They inform the workers on events in their home countries and about German industry and working conditions. They also bring entertainment and sport news.

"Immoral Co

Anglo-Saxons Are Betr
Civiliz

These are the words used by the Nationalist weekly, "Choque," about the cohabitation of barbarian Bolshevism and decadent Democracy." The article says:—

"Germany's mission in Europe is clear. Her task is to save the civilization of the old world from being flooded by wild Asia. In order to fulfil this mission, Germany must be strong. The Western Plutocracies, namely England and France, made efforts to prevent Germany from fulfilling this natural German task. If the Reich succeeded in overcoming these continual attacks it was certainly not a merit of the so-called

THE TRUTH ABOUT THIS WAR

BY

The Research Department of the British People's Party

"TO UNDERSTAND WAR WE MUST UNDERSTAND ITS UNDERLYING CAUSES."

(Continued from yesterday)

CHAPTER TWO

THE MILITARY ARMISTICE: PEACE TERMS: CONTEMPORARY COMMENT

The military armistice conditions were harsh; and included total German disarmament. Germany was thus rendered helpless and at the mercy of her enemies who were, nevertheless, bound by their acceptance of the Fourteen Points, on which Germany asked for the Armistice. The new democratic Germany relied entirely upon the honourable execution of President Wilson's Fourteen Points, accepted and agreed to by both sides, as forming the basis of peace. With her military strength reduced to nothing, however, as a prelude to the enforcement of peace terms she found her civic resistance destroyed for seven months after the Armistice by the blockade kept up by the Allies to starve her into acceptance, as Mr. Churchill has shown in his speech already quoted.

it. . . In the old law of the Church it was laid down that everyone must have a hearing, even the devil. *Etiam diabulus aiditur.* But the new democracy, which proposed to install the League of Nations, did not even obey the precept which the dark Middle Ages held sacred on behalf of the accused."

Germany was caught in a trap, she had no choice. Yielding to over-whelming force, the German Republic accepted the peace conditions. Then from all the civilised world a cry of anguish went up at the duplicity and double dealing of the victorious statesmen. It was described even then as one of the greatest betrayals in history.

Germany was presented with the peace terms as an ultimatum, which she repudiated as totally inconsistent with the conditions under which she laid down her arms.

The dictated peace was bad enough. What followed was worse. Every principle which the Fourteen Points had laid down as essential to permanent peace was contradicted in subsequent

Poland given control of the river and railway system and charge of the foreign affairs of the city, although not 5 per cent. of the inhabitants are of Polish descent. The Polish Corridor cut from Prussian territory, and cuts off East Prussia from the rest of Germany.

Memel district taken from Prussia, to be reserved by the Allies and disposed of by them as it suits their interests.

Abolition of the treaties which established political economy.

Annulment of all the treaties concluded by Germany during the war.

German-Austria formerly containing about 12 million German-Austrians reduced to a little State of hardly more than 6,000,000 inhabitants, about one-third of whom live in the capital. It cannot become united to Germany without the consent of the League of Nations, and is not allowed to participate in the affairs of another nation, namely of Germany, before being admitted to the League of Nations. As the consent of the League of Nations must be unanimous, a contrary vote site and conditions were appalling. Yet kindness could be shown at the very top even there (along with eccentricity). The three further destinations were in attractive places near the Swiss and Austrian borders.

Laufen, which housed unattached men, was in a converted Schloss: just across the river was the Austrian village of Obendorf where the carol *Silent Night, Holy Night* had been composed. The camp produced its own memorial volume, *The Bird Cage*, written in 1944 and published in 1945. Wurzach was a family camp which for some children and young people deported there had a holiday atmosphere. The third destination, a modern barracks in Biberach, a former *Strength Through Joy* centre, has been described most fully by the men, women and children who lived there. Many of the artefacts produced there have survived also. Some are beautiful, like decorated plates, tapestry and woodwork, others bizarre, like a ring made from false teeth plates, most ingenious, like toys made from tins.

Once in Biberach, as in the other camps, the deported Channel Islanders were expected to run their own organization, with a 'Camp Senior' as intermediary. There were not enough Germans to supervise or control them even if they had wished to do so. The messages they were able to send home via the Red Cross were often cheerful, though they often added that despite a round of camp activities, including concerts, sports and education classes, they were 'fed up'. 'We miss the gardening and the fishing here', one of them said, while her husband asked plaintively about 'the rabbits and birds'. Biberach even contrived to send home 300 pieces of soap and 500 tins of cocoa to Channel Islands children in March 1944.

With Red Cross food and other food and medical items from parcels the inhabitants of Biberach fared far better than those Channel Islanders who had been deported to penal camps for political offences; better indeed than the Channel Islanders they had left behind, particularly in the darkest days of 1944 before a Red Cross ship arrived.

What was most missed at first in the camps was also most missed in the Islands - a regular supply of 'real, true news'; and it was a historic day in Laufen when Frank Stroobant, its first Camp Senior - he was to give way to Sherwill - was able to listen to a BBC news bulletin on a 'Forbidden Whisper' radio, built laboriously by a Jerseyman, Billy Williams, largely from spare parts. Of course, other whispering never ceased. It was never easy to establish the truth.

FIVE Fortification

Hitler did not whisper, and it was under his direct orders that an elaborate system of fortifications was built in the Channel Islands. It was never completed, but fifty years later massive concrete towers, gun emplacements and bunkers still dominate parts of the shoreline. Some of the most extraordinary of the fortifications are to be found inland and below ground. The German word for fortification was *Festung*: it sounds attractive. And what are now called 'tunnels' the Germans called *Hohlgangsanlagen*, 'cave passage installations'. They were driven deep into the earth to serve as accommodation for stores, ammunition and equipment. The islands were heavily mined too, and there were extensive beach obstacles. By June 1942 there were 18,000 mines: by April 1944 there were 114,000.

It is not always easy for the uninitiated to identify which Channel Island fortifications were built by the Germans and which were built in periods of history before the Second World War. Fortification was not a new theme in Channel Islands history. Lieutenant-General Schmetzer, Inspector of

View through a periscope

Opposite: A German observation tower and wireless station, Corbière, Jersey

Achtung! Mines!

View of a harbour:
St Peter Port

Fortifications in the West, was impressed by earlier fortifications, which he believed were usually sited in the right strategic positions. All that they now needed was reinforced concrete. There were many new weapons, however, like the M19 automatic mortar mounted inside a steel cupola. There were several M19 bunker sites in Guernsey, one in Jersey and two in Alderney. Rudolf Graf von Schmettow, a nephew of Field-Marshal Rundstedt, had replaced Lanz in September 1940 and remained in post until February 1945.

Geological surveys had already been carried out before Hitler gave an order to increase the level of fortification in the Channel Islands, and this was before Germany's attack on the Soviet Union. As early as 2 June he

In defence of a beach

An anti-tank mine

had asked for maps of the Islands' defences, and plans of various kinds were devised. It is his order of 20 October, however, which has passed into history. While noting that 'operations on a large scale against the territories we occupy in the west are, as before, unlikely', Hitler forecast 'small-scale operations which might start 'at any moment', including a likely British attempt 'to regain possession of the Channel Islands'.

Barbed wire plus

Hitler thought in terms of permanent fortification, however, and not of immediate danger. The Channel Islands should never become British again: they would remain German to protect sea communication in the Channel. An impregnable fortress should be created with the utmost speed. 'The strength of the fortifications and the order in which they are erected' would be 'based on the principles and the practical knowledge gained from building the Western Wall.'

The wall to which Hitler then referred was not the Atlantic Wall, which was to figure so prominently in his long-term strategy, but the old Siegfried Line on Germany's western frontier. Yet his instructions were given not only to the High Command of the Army, which was to be responsible for 'the fortifications as a whole', but to the Navy and the Air Force. For the Army it was 'important to provide a close network of emplacements...sufficient for guns of a size capable of piercing armour plate 100 cm thick, to defend against tanks'. For the Navy 'one heavy battery' was required to supplement two on the French coast to safeguard sea approaches: this referred to what was to become the most striking and famous of the fortifications, the *Batterie Mirus* in Guernsey, 45,000 cubic metres of concrete, armed with four 30.5-centimetre guns with a range of 42 kilometres. For the Air Force 'strong points must be created with search lights'. 'Foreign labour, especially Russians and Spaniards but also Frenchmen' were to be used for the building works, and 'if necessary the civilian population could be conscripted'.

Plan of the Mirus Battery

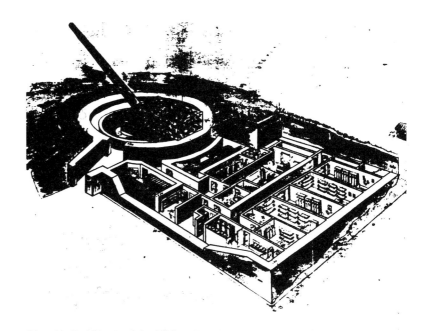

A German 22-cm gun:
Jerbourg

In the same month as the order was promulgated the Organization Todt, founded before the war to direct civilian labour, was given the task of assisting the Army in the fortification programme, and Dr Fritz Todt himself, as convinced as Hitler was that the Islands must remain German, paid a visit to Guernsey in November. Jersey now acquired the codename *Jakob*, Guernsey *Gustav* and Alderney *Adolf*; and under Todt's orders thousands of foreign workers poured into the islands. After the death of Todt in 1942 his organization was recast by Albert Speer, and in the spring of 1943 no fewer than 260,000 men were employed on the building of the Atlantic Wall. The purpose was primarily defensive as it had been in the case of the Siegfried Line: the offensive power of the wall lay in the concentration of

A naval gun from Russia

The Mirus control system

heavy coastal battery which could attack enemy ships. With control went camouflage. The Mirus looked like a farmhouse.

The implementation of the fortification programme demanded hours of deadening physical work, much of it by slave labour, employed in excavation as well as in building. It took a year and half, for example, to build the *Mirus* emplacements which included underground accommodation for 400 men. Yet implementation also demanded, even in the absence of sophisticated machinery, considerable technical skill at the top, and rested not only on physical labour but on standardized design. One other necessary requirement was improved transport of men and materials, and narrow-gauge railway lines were constructed in Jersey, Guernsey and Alderney, cutting through fields and gardens: if houses were in the way they were knocked down. The railways carried millions of tons of sand, cement, granite and steel. Wireless was another necessary mode of communication.

One of the most grandiose of projects was HO8, the intricate underground tunnel network in Jersey linking Meadowbank and Cap Verd. It involved the excavation of 43,900 tonnes of rock and the pouring of over 6000 square metres of concrete. There was almost a kilometre of corridors. The slave labour, working in the most treacherous of conditions, included Spanish Republicans (exiles from Franco's Spain who had escaped to France), Poles, Russians and Ukrainians. Those Channel Islanders who pitied them, sympathized with them, and when they escaped sheltered them, were treated as severely as the prisoners themselves. They were

Range-finding

Camouflage: a fake farmhouse

A German wireless station

Delving deep: the military hospital, Jersey

deported to German concentration camps, where some of them died.

Evacuated Alderney, where nearly 2500 men were at work in November 1941, was little more than a fortress, and its population greatly increased as a result of the entry of foreign workers in 1942 and 1943. Yet Alderney was also a nightmare prison island: there were 300 French Jews there in one camp in September 1943 and 700 Russians in another. They were barely clothed, dangerously underfed and appallingly treated. The Russian workers stationed on Alderney were said to be so weak that an Arab worker, about to leave the island to join the Foreign Legion, claimed that he could 'liquidate' 400 of them in an hour.

Underground hospital beds

The other side: Eric
Ravilious, *Channel Searchlights*

In fact, taking Guernsey as a whole, at least 15 Algerians themselves died
along with more than 42 Frenchmen. There was also one Chinese worker. No one, including most of the Germans, knew just what was going on,
and the silence was sometimes the silence of death. Over a hundred workers died in Alderney in the months of November and December 1942
alone.

What fortifications had been built there and in other Islands by October
1942 did not guarantee security. After British commando raids in
September - including Operation *Basalt*, a small scale raid on Sark - Hitler,
in conference with von Runstedt, Goering and Speer, mocked his advisers

On a Fortified Island: Edward
Ardizzone

A qualified apology

Telephone 2000

The Controlling Committee of the States of Guernsey.

Your Ref._____

In your reply
please quote Ref._____

HIRZEL HOUSE,
GUERNSEY.

Mr. Norman Le Tissier,   April 15th 1943.
Woodlawn, Castel.

Dear Sir,

    I very much regret to hear that your glasshouse
property was severely damaged by gunfire and that
this will result in considerable loss to you, and I
understand that your property was exceedingly well
cultivated. It does not appear to me that it would be
of much use having this property repaired, as there
is too much danger of similar damage every time these
big guns are fired. I therefore suggest that you grow
whatever you can in these greenhouses and you will not
thus be subjected to any cropping plan.

    You are entitled to submit a claim to the States
Supervisor for any loss incurred by you, and I suggest
that you do this. Should you require any further
information, please contact this office, or discuss
with my Inspector.

              Yours faithfully,

President,
Glasshouse Utilisation Board.
Copy to Mr.H.R.Bichard.

When the guns fire...

The ship that brought food -
and hope

who had told him the Channel Islands defences could not be broken. 'I am grateful to the English', he said, 'for proving me right by their various landing attempts. It shows up those who think I am always seeing phantoms, who say "Well, when are the English coming? There is absolutely nothing happening on the coast - we swim every day, and we haven't seen a single Englishman."'

There had been earlier complaints, however, from Runstedt and other generals that a disproportionate effort was being devoted to the fortification of the Channel Islands. And there was to be a heavy burden on manpower, military and civilian, as the total force reached above 40,000 in mid-1943. Thereafter fortifications work slowed down. As a result, the 'permanent' fortification scheme for the Channel Islands, lavish in scale as it had been, was left incomplete. The underground complex in Jersey, for example, was designed to have another 400 to 500 metres of tunnels. After D Day its use not as a depot but as a military hospital was carefully planned.

The isolation of the Islands increased after D Day when by a coincidence Schmettow was in conference with Runstedt at Rennes. He returned to

The parcels arrive

The parcels are distributed

Guernsey by boat on 7 June 1944. Allied advances by-passed the Channel Islands, and the main issue for the Germans then and thereafter was not the fortifications but food. It was just as critical an issue for the Channel Islanders also. Health and life itself depended on it.

In January 1945 the basic food ration was down to subsistence level: of 99 men who reported sick in Guernsey on the 13th day of that month 24 were suffering from malnutrition. There was now a new *Befehlshaber*, however: Vice-Admiral Friedrich Hüffmeier, a fervent Nazi, who after feuding with Schmettow, got rid of his chief (on health grounds) at the end of February 1945.

The Channel Islanders suffered more under the Hüffmeier regime than they ever had done before. Had it not been for Red Cross food parcels, brought in only after intricate secret negotiations in December 1944, they would have starved. And they were now subject to British bombing. There was an increase in robberies and in violence, even murders, and there were German soldiers, not Channel Islanders, who now were found guilty of sabotage. Yet the Germans, while reducing food rations, did not divert Red Cross food from the Islanders to themselves. And they suffered more than the Islanders did. Both were in desperate need of fuel also. 'There are many rumours of a Red Cross ship coming soon,' wrote Kathleen Nicole in her unpublished Guernsey diary on 3 November 1944; 'I wish it would hurry.'

The arrival, therefore, from Portugal of S.S. *Vega*, bearing food and medical supplies, was the happiest event for the Islanders between D Day and VE Day. Two days after Christmas 1944 100,000 food parcels were distributed, 4200 invalid diet parcels and, not least in importance, a consignment of soap. There were further deliveries in 1945. The *Vega* brought not only relief but hope, and it is scarcely surprising that one baby girl born at the time of its arrival was christened Vega.

In the House of Lords early in 1945 Lord Portsea, who always referred to the Channel Islands as the Royal Islands, attacked the British government for not having done more. He was not told, however, how difficult the diplomatic negotiations had been before the *Vega* sailed. For him and for many others in the Islands themselves 'liberation' would be 'redemption'. Meanwhile, Hüffmeier told his Forces that he would 'hold out here with you until final victory.'

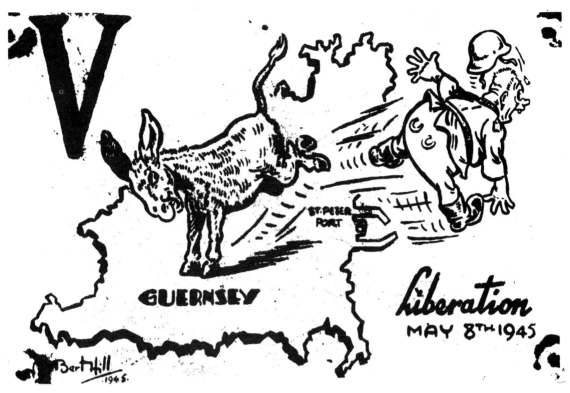

SIX Liberation

Tit for tat

Freedom at last!

Few weeks before liberation came, M.K. Weatherall, the Honorary Director of the Channel Islands Refugee Committee in England, wrote that the Channel Islanders now felt at last that liberation was imminent. Yet there were some curious final twists and turns of fortune. On the day the Americans entered Bonn in December 1944 Hüffmeier planned a bold German raid on the French port of Granville. Four Germans were killed, but 67 German prisoners of war being held there were released. One British prisoner taken, John Alexander, was the Principal Welfare Officer of UNRRA, the recently formed United Nations Relief and Rehabilitation Administration. Relief and rehabilitation were the Channel Islands issues that mattered most. A still-later twist was a reported broadcast by William Joyce, Lord Haw-Haw, on 9 April 1945. 'The BBC', he stated, 'is compelled to admire the strength of the German resistance in the west.'

Shock was the reaction, however, when five days later British troops entered the concentration camp at Belsen on 15 April 1945 and found around 35,000 corpses. One of the emaciated, living victims they also discovered was a Channel Islander, a young schoolteacher, Harold Le

September 1944: two versions of the news

Unconditional surrender on
HMS *Bulldog*

Announcing the end of the
occupation: Guernsey

Liberation Day in Jersey

A warm welcome

It's all over!

Druillenec: he had been sent there for radio offences. His sister, Mrs Louisa Gould, who had been arrested with him for sheltering two Russian prisoners and had been imprisoned at the concentration camp at Ravensbrück, had died in the gas chamber there. Another prisoner, the projectionist at the Jersey cinema, had made his way to Buchenwald. This was a sickening note with which to prepare for a joyous celebration.

The first event to set off the liberation sequence was Hitler's death on 1 May which brought the war to its climax. German flags in the Channel Islands flew at half-mast: Union Jacks were sold openly. There was so much excited speculation that on 6 May Coutanche had to appeal for calm. No measures, he urged, should be taken to antagonize the Germans. (Behind the scenes he secured the release of thirty political prisoners.)

'Everybody seems to think that the troops will come tomorrow' was a characteristic diary entry on 7 May. They did not arrive until two days later, but on 8 May the Bailiff addressed enthusiastic crowds outside the Royal Court building and at 3 pm introduced the public relay of a Churchill broadcast in which he movingly referred to 'our dear Channel Islands'. This would be 'the appropriate moment', the Bailiff added, 'for the raising of flags'. All restrictions on broadcasting were lifted, and King George VI would be broadcasting that evening at 9 pm.

In equally appropriate language, of which Churchill would have approved, Dorothy Higgs wrote in her Guernsey diary: 'We are alive and well and BRITISH again.' A special meeting of the States had been convened that day, and a special single-sheet edition of the *Guernsey Star* was

Below left. On the way home: 'marching' out

On the way home: under orders

On the way home: out to sea

Food at last - from Britain

Plenty to take!

A family at peace: the Williams
family of St Peter Port,
Guernsey

published. Churchill's speech was greeted with the same acclamation as in Jersey.

Hüffmeier, stubbornly determined – he had threatened to blow up all German arms and ammunition – did not surrender formally until 9 May, seven hours after the official end of the war in Europe, and it was on that day that the Channel Islands saw their first British uniformed troops. There were parting formalities as the Germans handed over: 'we faced each other with polite but wordless bows', wrote von Aufsess, 'like so many Chinese mummers'. A Combined Press correspondent who watched the British arrive in Guernsey described the 'scenes of delirious joy' in St Peter Port which he found almost heart-breaking. 'These people who have been eating rabbit skins, getting 1½ lbs of potatoes a week, who had that morning breakfasted on stewed cabbage leaves' were now free again. 'One man told me he was smoking a cigarette for which he had paid 28s. I offered him one, and in a frenzied grabbing of hands the packet of cigarettes disappeared.... Perhaps their one consolation was that the German garrison was even worse off.'

Alderney's liberation did not take place until 16 May, and it was not until 20 May that 2332 German prisoners of war were taken away from the island. They left from a pier built by the Germans, who had once hoped that it would be the disembarkation point for the invasion of Britain.

The officer in charge of the Hampshire Regiment, which landed in Jersey on 10 May, told the crowds as the troops came ashore, accompanied by RAF aeroplanes in the skies, 'We would have been here a long time ago, boys, only it would have meant bombing you to Hell'. They are words that stick fifty years later: more so, perhaps, than the words of Herbert Morrison, the Home Secretary, who on 14 and 15 May told the Islanders when he visited them that 'there was never a moment when we forgot you'. One of the men who accompanied him was the Home Office civil servant Markbreiter, who had been at the other end of the telephone line between London and the Channel Islands in 1940.

Charles V. Gardner wrote the words and composed the music of a hymn that best expressed the feelings of those many Channel Islanders who were interested in more than cigarettes. It was one of many verse compositions written by Channel Islanders during the war:

> Dark were the days we called in fear
> 'Help us, oh Lord! our cross to bear!'
> 'Neath the Invaders' heel we lay,
> Loved ones growing weaker day-by-day ...
> Now thank we, Lord, for all Thy Love!
> Dark days are over! Sun above.

New visitors to Sark

SEVEN Summers to come

There was much talk in May 1945 of a 'return to normal', not least on 12 May, declared a public holiday. Nonetheless, as many Channel Islanders at home or in Britain had warned, it would not be possible to return to summers like that of 1939. Too much had changed. In many respects Britain itself had changed even more. And soon Churchill, who to the regret of the Channel Islanders never visited them in 1945, heavily lost the first British general election for ten years.

A Channel Islands study group, based in Britain, had published a report on the future of the Islands in March 1944, *Nos Iles*. One of its most interesting sections was on tourism. There was 'a much larger potential for tourism than before, but it would demand enterprise to satisfy it'. The tourists returned in 1947 and 1948, and their numbers were to grow.

The Guernsey Chamber of Commerce, when it reassembled in 1945, talked of penicillin and commercial radio, not of tourists - or of bunkers. There was certainly little thought then in Guernsey or Jersey that Germans would be amongst the tourists of the future or that the fortifications that they had left behind them would one day draw in British tourists. The fortifications were thought of as eyesores, and efforts were made in both Jersey and Guernsey to dispose at once of all that was disposable as scrap metal: George Dawson made a fortune out of dealing in it. Not everyone approved, but clearing quickly began.

There was so much to clear, however, and so much that was impossible to destroy, that eyesores remained. So, too, did memories, memories not only of the Germans - and many effigies of Guy Fawkes during the November the Fifths of the 1960s were dressed in German uniforms - but of each other. For all the relief, the Occupation had left a taint, as it did in all occupied countries. There had been violation of community as well as of soil.

The Duchess of Kent greets those who escaped

In Alderney, where there were few memories, the immediate aftermath was different. The island that had been abandoned was in an appalling state - for example, the pews had been ripped out of the church and it had to be restored with the help of voluntary effort from outside. The WVS responded magnificently to the immediate need, carefully and precisely calculating just how many beds (188), blankets (720), kettles (300), electric irons (3) and books ('mainly light fiction') would be needed when the exiles returned. After the Islanders were all resettled - and old boundaries had been identified - the WVS renewed its association with them in a different way: its members in another British island, the Isle of Wight, embroidered a carpet and provided ecclesiastical furnishing.

Who then would have thought that the latest 1990s tourist booklet on

The removal of a 22,500-gallon fuel tank, 1947

Alderney, which since 1945 has attracted many new residents, among them the late John Arlott, would tell its readers to 'imagine a lovely village - a very special sort of village almost totally unaffected by the outside world'? Time has rolled back there to 1939.

Or has it? In Alderney there are even more fortifications spanning the centuries than in the other Islands, and they are as much a source of interest as they are in Jersey and Guernsey, where on the occasion of the 40th anniversary of liberation Military Vehicle Conservation Groups staged displays and postal historians explained just why *Feldpost* history was as absorbing a pursuit as Post Office history. A Channel Islands Study Circle, later called the Channel Islands Specialists' Society, had been set up in 1950 - with its own bulletin, and in 1972 its President, Bill Newport, had published his book *The Stamps and Postal History of the Channel Islands*.

Clearing a bunker

Children, not consultants, led the way to a change in attitudes towards the legacy of the German occupation, although as early as Easter 1946 the Underground Military Hospital in Jersey was opened to the public. Ten years later, two Guernsey schoolboys, Richard Heaume and John Robinson, formed a 'club' to collect occupation relics, including helmets and gas masks, from bunkers, tunnels and slit trenches. Stirred with a sense of curiosity and adventure, they embarked on an often dangerous and always dirty exploration in defiance of many of their elders, including their headmaster.

By 1961 the size of Richard Heaume's collection had grown so substantially that it could not be contained in his attic. So, too, had the membership of his club, the Society for the Preservation of German Occupation Relics, which at the start consisted mainly of pupils of Elizabeth College. The name was shortened to the German Occupation Society in 1963, and the word 'German' was dropped in 1970. Three years later, Heaume opened his private Occupation Museum to the public. So, too, did a fellow enthusiast in Jersey, Richard Mayne. A main theme of the Society

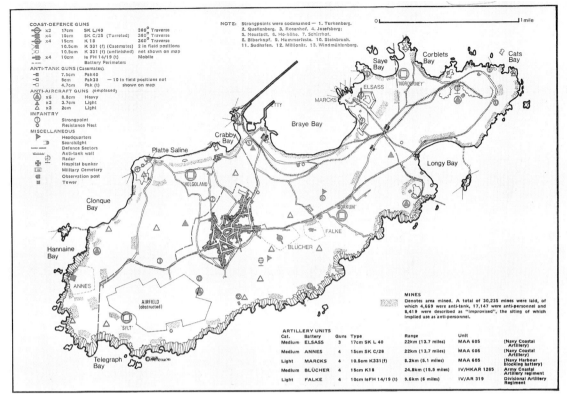

Alderney as a fortress island, 1980

from the start was conservation, which was soon to become a favourite pursuit in other parts of Britain.

A landmark date was 1966 when in August the Society's first Newsletter was circulated and the first rules were drafted. The Newsletter was the *Channel Islands Occupation Review*, edited in alternate years from Jersey and Guernsey. The 1973 number was the first to include photographs: the 1974 number was the first to be professionally printed. It also included an index.

Great use was made of photographs. Many of them tell a story, and since photography was a pastime that the Germans had greatly enjoyed during the years of occupation they told German as well as Channel Islander stories. The Society welcomed foreign members, including Germans, some of whom now come back to look at old sites they knew and to trace old people that they had known. Some had written poems while they served in the Islands, praising their skies and their seas. Some visitors, however, are former prisoners of war who led the grimmest of existences while they lived, as the Islanders themselves did, 'under the jackboot'.

Meanwhile, there have been continuing reminders of war, some of them bizarre. A set of Guernsey occupation Reichsmarks was stolen from the German Occupation Museum in 1976. A whole packet of wrapped Sauerkraut was found in 1977. In 1993 a large 500lb bomb (5ft x 2ft diameter) was found in Guernsey on the sea bed 500 yards from the St Peter Port Harbour Signal Station. The bomb was exploded by a Royal Navy underwater clearance team. Lest we forget.

Studying German fortifications
at St Malo

Memorial to the Slave
Workers, Alderney

Collecting the artefacts: a
German NCO tunic

A new tapestry

APPENDIX 1 What to see

Both Jersey and Guernsey provide information leaflets. The most interesting site in Jersey is the privately owned German Underground Hospital, rightly described by Jack Higgins as a 'time capsule of the occupation'. At the end of long corridors the visitor reaches the unique Miere Collection, 'one man's record of the Island's resistance'. The privately owned Channel Islands Military Museum with interesting artefacts is located in an original and restored bunker next to Microworld, St Ouen. See also the Jersey Museum in St Helier, the German observation post and defences at Elizabeth Castle, and the underground bunker at La Hougue Bie, a prehistoric monument. Notes on 'Bunker Hunting' figure regularly in the *Channel Islands Occupation Review*: they include the necessary warning that most bunkers, gun-pits and defences are on private property.

Guernsey's approach to fortifications spans the centuries, and recommendations set out in an independent 1989 report on the future of tourism in Guernsey. The Guernsey Tourist Board, working in co-operation with the Heritage Committee, began a 'Fortress Guernsey' project which is 'dedicated to the preservation and interpretation of two thousand years of the Bailiwick's history'. One of its brochures, *Guernsey's German Fortifications*, is a useful brief guide to what occupation fortifications to see, including coastal batteries, direction-finding towers and command posts, some of which are now undergoing restoration. One fascinating site, Vale Castle, occupied by the Germans during the War, had been an iron age hillfort. The castle is believed to be fifteenth-century, and the defences were strengthened in the eighteenth century.

Richard Heaume's German Occupation Museum is packed with treasures, including rare occupation artefacts: it also presents film material based on British and German archives. There are other valuable relics in the La Valette Military Underground Museum, located in one of Guernsey's 41 tunnel sites. Designed to be a fuel store, it was converted into a museum between December 1987 and August 1988.

There is no complete guide to film and video (or to oral) records. Much is in private hands, much in the Imperial War Museum. Privately made and owned films include Olive Thompson's secret filming of occupation troops, the photographer Wilfred Le Cheminant's colour film of the liberation of Jersey, and Dr Sutcliffe's colour film of the liberation of Guernsey.

In Alderney the small but interesting Alderney Society Museum, located in an old eighteenth-century school, houses an interesting collection of finds. The Alderney Ordnance Survey map (1988) depicts both British and German defences in considerable detail. The island has the only remaining working passenger transport railway in the Channel Islands.

Sark is as interesting to the visitor of the 1990s (British or German) as it was to the Germans between 1940 and 1945; and it now has its own small occupation museum.

APPENDIX 2 What to read

C. Cruickshank's *The German Occupation of the Channel Islands* (Alan Sutton, 1975) is an indispensable, well-researched official history (paperback illustrated edition, 1993) which does not shirk criticism of official policies. It makes use of the war files of the Bailiff in Jersey and of the Controlling Committee in Guernsey; of Prime Minister's and Cabinet papers and papers of (among other bodies) the Home Office, the Admiralty, the Air Staff, Coastal Command, Combined Operations and the Directorate of Military Operations in the Public Record Office in London. Since 1975 more files have been opened, particularly Home Office and Guernsey files in 1993 and 1994.

There are parallel German Military Government files in the Bundesarchiv, Freibourg, which were used by Cruickshank, and at Coblenz there is a huge collection of photographs which even now has never been fully explored. The papers cover both military command and civil administration and include German Naval Historical Branch papers. Cruickshank also consulted microfilms of papers, including captured documents, in the National Archives of the United States and SHAEF papers.

There are several unofficial illustrated histories of the occupation which are revealing and readable; some of them have gone through different (including revised) editions, sometimes with different publishers, and sometimes widened in scope. The chronological order in which they appeared is of great importance given the history of shifting post-1945 attitudes to the war and occupation and the uncovering of new evidence. For this reason, the details of the first editions are given: A. and M.S. Woods, *Islands in Danger* (Evans Brothers, 1955); C. Toms, *Hitler's Fortress Islands* (New English Library, 1967); F.W. Falla, *The Silent War* (Leslie Frewin Ltd., 1967); P. King, *The Channel Islands War* (Robert Hale, 1991). L.P. Sinel's *The German Occupation of Jersey* (Jersey Evening Post, 1945) should be compared with the unpublished version and a 1984 edition (La Haule Books).

See also: R. Mollet, *The German Occupation of Jersey, 1940-1945* (Société Jersiaise, 1954); and H.R.S. Pocock (ed.), *The Memoirs of Lord Coutanche, A Jerseyman Looks Back* (Phillimore, 1975). For Guernsey see J.C. Sauvary, *Diary of the German Occupation of Guernsey, 1940-1945* (Self Publishing Association, 1990). The files of the *Jersey Evening Post* and the *Guernsey Evening Press* are both indispensable.

Sonia Hillson has compiled an illuminating volume of memories, *Jersey, Occupation Remembered* (Jarrold, 1986). For one of the most remarkable of Channel Islanders see: S. Hathaway, *Dame of Sark* (Heinemann, 1961); B. Stoney, *Sibyl Dame of Sark, A Biography* (Hodder and Stoughton, 1978); and X. Franks, *War on Sark: The Secret Letters of Julia Tremayne* (Webb and Bower, 1981).

For German evidence see the files of the *Deutsche Guernsey Zeitung* and *Deutsche Inselzeitung*; Sonderführer Dr Hans Auerbach, *Die Kanalinseln: Jersey, Guernsey, Sark* (published by the order of the Commanding Officer, Jersey, spring of 1942); Dr Bessenrodt, *Die Insel Alderney* (Deutsche Guernsey Zeitung, 1942); G. Nebel, *Bei den Nördlichen Hesperiden* (Wuppertel, 1948); and *The von Aufsess Occupation Diary*, edited and translated by K.J. Nowlan (Phillimore, 1985). See also the privately published study of D. Dalmau, *Slave Worker in the Channel Islands* (1954). Cruickshank refers to an interesting report on the Islands by Karl Heinz Pfeffer, a professor who visited them in 1941. Later, the British produced *Nachrichten für die Truppe* for German soldiers.

For a book of illustrations with text by R. Mayne with *légendes en français* see *Channel Islands Occupied* (Jarrold, n.d.), 'dedicated to the memory of the known 557 slave workers, mainly Russian and Spanish, who died in these islands between 1942 and 1944'. See also *The German Occupation of Jersey 1940-1945: Reference Maps with Supporting Text and Comprehensive History* by H.B. Baker (n.d.).

Early books published soon after the end of the war include (in chronological order): R. Mollet, *Jersey under the Swastika* (Hyperion Press, 1945); H. Wyatt, *Jersey in Jail* (Ernest Huelin, 1945); A.H. Downer, *The Channel Island Schools* (Jersey Evening Post, 1946); K. Durand, *Guernsey under German Rule* (The Guernsey Society, 1946); R. Grandin, *Smiling Through* (Jersey Evening Post, 1946); R.C.F. Maugham, *Jersey under the Jackboot* (W.H. Allen, 1946); V. Cortvriend, *Isolated Island* (Guernsey Evening Press, 1947); D. Higgs, *Guernsey Diary* (Linden, Lewis Ltd, 1947); V. Coysh, *Swastika Over Guernsey* (The Guernsey Press Co., 1955); M. Marshall, *Hitler Invades Sark* (Guernsey Press, 1963); and P. Le Sauteur, *Swastika Over Jersey* (Streamline Publications, 1968).

Later books, published before Cruickshank, include (in chronological order): M. St. J. Packe and M. Dreyfus, *The Alderney Story, 1939-1949* (The Alderney Society and Museum, 1971); and R. Mayne, *Channel Islands Occupied* (Jarrold and Sons, 1972).

J.K. Antill produced *A Bibliography of the German Occupation of Jersey and other Channel Islands in 1975* (Jersey States Greffe). It requires to be up-dated given the subsequent publication (in alphabetical order) of: W. Bell, *Guernsey Green* (The Guernsey Press Co., 1992); M. Bihet, *A Child's War* (The Guernsey Press Co., 1985) and *Reflections of Guernsey* (The Guernsey Press, 1993); B. Bonnard, *Island of Dread in the Channel* (Alan Sutton, 1991) and *Alderney at War* (Alan Sutton, 1993); G.B. Edwards, *The Book of Ebenezer Le Page* (Hamish Hamilton, 1981); R. Harris, *Islanders Deported* (CISS Publishing, 1979); M. Mahy, *There is an Occupation* (Guernsey Press Ltd, 1992); R. McLoughlin and C. Smeaton, *The First Casualty* (Sanctuary Inns Ltd, 1991); T.X.B. Pantcheff, *Alderney, Fortress Island* (Phillimore, 1981); C.W. Partridge, *Hitler's Atlantic Wall* (D.I. Publications, 1976); C. Partridge and J. Warbridge, *Mirus, The Making of a Battery* (Ampersand Press Ltd, 1983); C. Partridge and T. Davenport, *The Fortifications of Alderney* (Alderney Publishers, 1993); and S.H. Steckoll, *The Alderney Death Camp* (Granada, 1982).

The Government Printers, Guernsey have published under the guidance of Peter Dobson a number of booklets with packs, the first of them by June Money, *Aspects of War: Entertainments and Pastimes* (1993). See also W.G. Ramsay, *The War on the Channel Islands - Then and Now* (Battle of Britain Prints International, n.d.).

Important material is to be found in the successive volumes of the *Bulletins* of the Société Jersiaise, the *Reports and Transactions* of the Société Guernesiaise and the annual numbers of the *Channel Islands Occupation Review*. There are large numbers of unpublished reminiscences, some recorded on tape.

For the long-term history of the Channel Islands, including constitutional and geopolitical history, see: J.H. Le Patourel, *The Medieval Administration of the Channel Islands* (Oxford University Press, 1938); and 'The Political Development of the Channel Islands' in *Transactions of La Société Guernesiaise* (1946); R. Lemprière, *Portrait of the Channel Islands* (Hale, 1970; 5th edn. 1990); W.D. Hooke, *The Channel Islands* (Hale, 1953); G.R. Balleine, *A History of the Island of Jersey* (P. Staples, 1950); C.P. Le Huray, *The Bailiwick of Guernsey* (Haughtier and Stoughton, 1952); Sir John Loveridge, *The Constitution and Law of Guernsey* (La Société Guernesiaise, 1975); A.R. De Carteret and A.H. Ewen, *The Fief of Sark* (Guernsey Press, 1969); and M. Marshall, *Sark* (Guernsey Press, 1961).

For the larger story of the Second World War see P. Calvocoressi, G. Wint and J. Pritchard, *Total War: The Causes and Courses of the Second World War* (Allen Lane, 1972), although it does not mention the Channel Islands; M. Gilbert (biographer of Winston Churchill), *Second World War* (Weidenfeld, 1989), which does; B. Collier, *The Defence of the United Kingdom* (HMSO, 1957); P. Seal, *Fortress Europe* (Airlife, 1988); H. Zimmermann, *Der Atlantikwall* (Schild-Verlag GmbH, 1989); P. Gamelin, *Le Mur de l'Atlantique: Les Blockhaus de l'Illusoire* (Daniel et Cie, 1974); S.W. Mitcham, *Hitler's Legions* (Dorset Press, 1985); A.J.P. Taylor, *English History, 1914-1945* (Oxford University Press, 1965); A. Marwick, *Britain in the Century of Total War* (The Bodley Head, 1968); A. Calder, *The People's War: Britain, 1939-1945* (Cape, 1969); and S. Briggs, *Keep Smiling Through* (Weidenfeld, 1975). M.E. Bunting, *The Model Occupation* (Harper Collins, 1995) appeared after my book was complete.

APPENDIX 3 People to thank

My thanks are due to the many people who have contributed to our understanding of this unique period in British history. The Channel Islands are sometimes thought of as marginal in relation to the history of the Second World War as a whole, but they were central, not marginal, to the people who lived through it. They were not marginal either to Hitler.

My book could not have been written had not many other people written earlier about the topics that it covers: these figure in my list of books to read. I have met some, but not most, of their authors. Some are now dead. The time will come when memory ceases to be the key to the interpretation of the story. For this reason alone historians of the future will owe a great debt to the Channel Islands Occupation History Society.

My own particular debts in relation to my own book are to:

the Bailiffs of Jersey and Guernsey, Sir Peter Crill, who escaped from his Island by boat in November 1944 and landed on the Normandy coast before going up to Oxford, and Sir Graham Dorey;

Ken Tough, H.M. Greffier and Secretary of the Channel Islands Occupation Society (Guernsey), who introduced me to key documents and provided long-term perspectives;

Colin Partridge, Chairman of the Channel Islands Occupation Society (Guernsey), military historical consultant to the Guernsey Tourist Board - and much else, who made an all-too-brief visit to Alderney an occasion of great excitement and who has kindly read through my text;

W. M. Ginns, Secretary, Channel Islands Occupation Society (Jersey), whose memories are still vivid and who has produced scholarly work on fortification and occupation; and M. and J.A. Ginns;

Richard Heaume for his wealth of knowledge, generously placed at my disposal, and, above all, for his pioneering work in saving the past;

Peter and Paul Balshaw, creators of the Underground Military Museum, Guernsey, who showed me many interesting historical items;

John Goodwin, learned Archivist, Channel Islands Occupation Society Guernsey, who revealed treasures in his own home;

Carel Toms, who following after Alan and Mary Wood opened up Channel Islands occupation history to non-Channel Islanders;

Hugh Lenfestey, learned Archivist, States of Guernsey, who introduced me to an archive rich in documentation;

Rona Cole, Director of Museums, Guernsey, who sadly died a few days after I saw the Museum with her and talked to her about the past;

Dr Harry Tomlinson, Librarian of the Priaulx Library, who identified for me several useful papers about the Islands before and after the War;

Molly Bihet for her intimate and revealing personal stories;

Bill Green, a gentle-man, whose memoirs wisely fit the occupation years which he lived through, into a longer personal history;

Joe Miere, who made a visit to the Underground Hospital in Jersey one of the most remarkable days in my life. He knows the details of hundreds of occupation stories and keeps in touch with the subjects of many of them. He was curator of the German Underground Hospital from 1976 to 1991;

M.P. Costard, reviews editor of the Channel Islands Occupation Society, Jersey;

Michael Day, Director of the Jersey Museum and other members of his staff, particularly Doug Ford and Wayne Audrain; The Société Jersiaise, for access to information and archives;

Audrey Lobb, who was at school with my sister and who has sent me Jersey information based on oral interviews and videotape;

The Presidents of the Tourist Boards of Jersey and Guernsey, Senator R. Shenton and Deputy Geoff Norman, and their colleagues and, in particular, Evan Ozanne, Mike Tate and Senator J. Le Maistre for their delightful hospitality as well as for their help;

Christopher Dowling, Penny Ritchie Calder, Carolyn Marsden–Smith, Lisa Douglas, and other members of the staff of the Imperial War Museum without whom this book would not have been written;

Susan Hard, who has worked with me on many books and who lived in the Channel Islands after the war;

Timothy Auger of Batsford, who has been of immense help in bringing the illustrated text through the press along with other members of the Batsford office, in particular Alison Struckett and Vaughan Collinson;

and, above all, Pat Spencer, who word-processed various drafts of this text at the greatest possible speed and with inimitable patience.

Picture acknowledgements

All the photographs in the book are from the collection of The Imperial War Museum, London, and are reproduced with their permission, with the exception of the following, for which grateful acknowledgement is made:

The Alderney Society, pages 26 and 87

Susan Briggs, page 88 (middle)

Royal Pavilion, Art Gallery and Museum, Brighton, 69 (bottom), 70 (top)

The Channel Islands Occupation Review (1988), page 17

W. M. and J. A. Ginns, pages 86 (bottom left), 88 (top)

Jersey Evening Post, page 12; and page 88 (bottom left)

Jersey Museum, pages 34, 44 (top), 46, 47 (top), 49 (bottom), 54, 55, 77 (top), 78 (bottom), 85, 88 (bottom right)

La Valette Underground Military Museum, pages 42 (top), 65 (bottom), 86 (top)

ECPA, Paris (cover photograph; print courtesy of Channel Islands Occupation Society)